STUDIES IN MEDITERRANEAN ARCHAEOLOGY

VOL. LXIII

Applications of Technical Devices in Archaeology

THE USE OF X-RAYS, MICROSCOPE, ELECTRICAL AND ELECTRO-MAGNETIC DEVICES AND SUBSURFACE INTERFACE RADAR

BY

PETER M. FISCHER

GÖTEBORG 1980
PAUL ÅSTRÖMS FÖRLAG

Abstract

Eine Untersuchung der Kieferfragmente und Zähne aus zwei Gräbern von Trypes bei Dromolaxia, Cypern

A number of jaw fragments and teeth from two Late Cypriote Bronze Age tombs from Trypes near Dromolaxia have been investigated. The diagnostic methods used were X-rays, direct inspection and microscope. The main points of the investigation were the diagnosis of caries, periodontal disease, mineralisation defects and attrition. Minimum number and age of the buried individuals has been estimated: Eight children between 1.5 and 14 years and nine adults.

The Jaws and Teeth of a Late Bronze Age Skeleton from Hala Sultan Tekke, Cyprus

The examined material from a Late Cypriote Bronze Age shaft grave from Hala Sultan Tekke consisted of parts of the upper and lower jaws including 30 teeth, some of which were broken. The material has been examined by X-rays and direct inspection with particular attention to dental conditions, a rough age determination and the state of health and habits on the basis of dental conditions. One possible caries lesion, periodontal disease and severe dental attrition could be seen. A rough estimate of the individual's age is 30–40 years. Some possible diseases have been discussed.

Resistivity Measurements at Hala Sultan Tekke, Cyprus

Electrical prospecting was performed at Hala Sultan Tekke, Cyprus, using a "Geohm" instrument, in 1979. The purpose of the electrical resistivity survey was: 1. to determine if it is possible to carry out electrical prospecting under the dry summertime conditions at Hala Sultan Tekke, 2. to compare the possible results with the results obtained by a differential proton magnetometer used in 1972, 3. to compare the possible results with the preliminary excavation results, and 4. to search for the city wall.

It has been verified that electrical prospecting is possible. A comparison with magnetic prospecting is largely in agreement; however, differences did occur. The results made it possible to give a detailed experimental interpretation that was in reasonable agreement with succeeding excavations. The search for the city wall, however, was fruitless.

The Use of a Metal Detector in Archaeology

During the campaign in 1978 at Hala Sultan Tekke, the Swedish Cyprus Expedition used the C-Scope TR 400/500 metal detector. The detector tested an area of about 2000 m² and indicated 22 metal objects between 40.0 x 5.0 cm and 0.7 x 0.5 cm in size. It indicated the presence of bronze, copper, gold, iron and lead. The finds were located both "on surface" and down to 10 cm beneath the surface.

The detector even revealed the presence of limestone in blocks and crushed form and cavities were also indicated.

Geophysical Prospecting at Hala Sultan Tekke, Cyprus

During the 1979 season of excavation of the Late Cypriote Bronze Age town at Hala Sultan Tekke, the writer carried out an electro-magnetic survey with the help of a Very Low Frequency Discriminative Detector (VLF-Discriminator). The survey resulted in the discovery of a rich shaft grave and in an area of some 10,000 sq.m., 159 metal artifacts (bronze, copper, gold, iron, lead and silver) as well as some non-metal objects and features. Comparisons were made with two other electro-magnetic devices, a Pulsed Induction (PIM) and an Induction Balance (IB) detector. The tests favoured the VLF detector.

Electro-Magnetic Detectors
Technical Principles and Field Trials

The present article gives a short description of the basic technical principles of the most common electro-magnetic devices: Beat Frequency Oscillator (BFO), Induction Balance (IB) – Transmit-Receive (TR), Pulsed Induction (PIM) and Very Low Frequency (VLF-Discriminator). Advantages and disadvantages and the approximate depth penetration of these detectors as derived from field trials are shown.

The Use of a Soil Conductivity Meter (SCM) at Hala Sultan Tekke, Cyprus

During the 1980 excavation season of the Late Cypriote Bronze Age town at Hala Sultan Tekke, a survey of some 4000 m² with a Soil Conductivity Meter (SCM) was performed. Only shallow buried features were detected, providing an indistinct indication of these features. The SCM can not be seen as a substitute for electrical resistivity measurements or magnetic prospecting.

Subsurface Interface Radar Survey at Hala Sultan Tekke, Cyprus

During the 1980 excavation season at Hala Sultan Tekke, Cyprus, a Subsurface Interface Radar (SIR) survey of some 5000 m² was performed using a device built by Geophysical Survey System Incorporated (GSSI), Hudson N.H., U.S.A. 900 MHz and 400 MHz antennas were used. The 400 MHz antenna, with an approximate penetration of 2 m, was preferable to the 900 MHz antenna with a lesser penetration. Significant radar echoes were directly marked on the ground and checked by test trenches, which revealed walls or blocks of stones and metal finds with pin-point accuracy.

Fischer P.M., Applications of Technical Devices in Archaeology, The Use of X-rays, Microscope, Electrical and Electro-Magnetic Devices and Subsurface Interface Radar, 64 pages, *Studies in Mediterranean Archaeology*, Vol. LXIII, Göteborg 1980. Published by Professor Paul Åström, Johannebergsgatan 24, S-412 55 Gothenburg, Sweden. Thesis from the Department of Ancient Culture and Civilisation, Gothenburg University.
Key words: Teeth and archaeology, archaeological prospecting (electrical, electro-magnetic and radar).

ISBN 91 85058 33 5   Printed in Sweden   Gotab, Kungälv 1980

CONTENTS

PREFACE

This study consists of two articles dealing with the dental investigations of archaeological materials from Cyprus and six articles concerning archaeological prospecting carried out at Hala Sultan Tekke, Cyprus. In both investigations technical devices were used.

The use of X-rays in dental investigations is routine so this method and the microscope used in the histopathological investigation are helpful tools in confirming or denying the diagnosis made by direct inspection of an archaeological material.

The geophysical techniques used at Hala Sultan Tekke were electrical resistivity and electro-magnetic surveys. The electrical resistivity survey is a method often used in archaeological field work. At Hala Sultan Tekke it was used in order to compare with and to complement the magnetic survey performed by R. E. Linington in 1972. The purposes of the electro-magnetic surveys were:

1. The evaluation of advanced electro-magnetic detectors (s.c. "metal detectors")

2. The evaluation of a Soil Conductivity Meter (SCM) as well as a comparison to the electrical resistivity and the subsurface radar surveys.

3. The test of a Subsurface Interface Radar, a recently developed method with archaeological applications. To the author's knowledge this radar survey is perhaps the first successful survey of its kind in the Mediterranean area.

The articles "Eine Untersuchung der Zähne und Kieferfragmente aus zwei Gräbern von Trypes bei Dromolaxia, Cypern" and "The Use of a Metal Detector in Archaeology" have been published in *Opuscula Atheniensia* XIII. The article "Geophysical prospecting at Hala Sultan Tekke, Cyprus" is at press with the *Journal of Field Archaeology (JFA)* 7 (1980), Boston University. The tables in the "Appendix" to the above article which were not printed in the JFA due to lack of printing space reveal a description of all metal finds discovered by the electro-magnetic detector and those metal finds discovered during the excavations but not indicated by the detector. In the above article ("Geophysical Prospecting at Hala Sultan Tekke, Cyprus") the section about electrical prospecting refers to the survey which is described in detail in the article "Resistivity Measurements at Hala Sultan Tekke, Cyprus".

I wish to thank all those who have given me their kind support. Mr. Håkan Wallin, director of the engineering firm "Wakebo", has lent me some electro-magnetic devices and has given me valuable advice in using them to maximum advantage. Members of the Swedish Cyprus Expedition, especially Mr. Rickard and Lennart Åström, and several Cypriote students helped with the surveys. The radar survey was possible thanks to excellent cooporation with the Department of Engineering Geology, Lund Institute of Technology. Thanks also to the JFA who have been kind enough to print my article about geophysical prospecting. The playwright Donovan O'Malley and Engineer Rodrick Sutherland have helped with my English. The photographs were taken by Mr. Bo Gabrielsson, Mr. Jan Thyrén and Mrs. Nina Witzel.

Above all, my great appreciation to Professor Paul Åström who has supported my work with his advice and encouragement and provided the necessary financial help especially concerning the expensive radar survey. He has also undertaken the publication in *Studies in Mediterranean Archaeology*. Professor Paul Åström's recognition of the value of technical devices supporting and facilitating field archaeological work is worthy of emulation.

Finally I wish to express my thanks to my wife Ingrid for her infinite patience throughout this project.

Göteborg, October 1980

Peter M. Fischer

ISBN 91-85086-33-9

6

EINE UNTERSUCHUNG DER KIEFERFRAGMENTE UND ZÄHNE AUS ZWEI GRÄBERN VON TRYPES BEI DROMOLAXIA, CYPERN

VON

PETER M. FISCHER

EINLEITUNG

Im Juli 1977 wurde mir die Auszeichnung erteilt, an der schwedischen Cypernexpedition, die bei Hala Sultan Tekke gräbt, teilnehmen zu dürfen. Bei dieser Gelegenheit entdeckten Teilnehmer der schwedischen Cypernexpedition zwei Gräber in einem Sandhügel, Trypes genannt, ca 1 km westlich von Hala Sultan Tekke und ca ½ km nördlich des kleinen Dorfes Dromolaxia.[1] Dieser Hügel wurde als Sandgrube verwendet, und bei Schachtarbeiten wurden zwei Gräber geöffnet.[2] Nachdem diese Arbeiten gestoppt worden waren, durfte ich aktiv an der Ausgrabung dieser beiden Gräber teilnehmen.

Das östliche der beiden Gräber — als Grab I bezeichnet — enthielt Keramik, die nach einer vorläufigen Schätzung der jüngeren spätcyprischen Bronzezeit angehört, (eventuell spätcyprisch II, 1425—1190 v. Chr.)[3] Das westliche Grab — als Grab II bezeichnet und einige Meter vom östlichen entfernt — enthielt dagegen Keramik, die vorläufig der älteren spätcyprischen Bronzezeit zuzuschreiben wäre (eventuell spätcyprisch I, 1575—1425 v. Chr.).[3]

Da das Risiko vorlag, dass Unbefugte die während der Nacht unbewachten Gräber zerstören konnten, wurde die Ausgrabung in grosser Eile durchgeführt. Das führte dazu, dass zwar die Keramik und andere Funde aus den beiden Gräbern separat registriert wurden, die Knochen — und Zähnefunde allerdings zu Beginn dieser Ausgrabung gemeinsam eingeordnet wurden. Erst später registrierte man auch diese Funde separat. Diese Untersuchung besteht deswegen aus drei Teilen: Die Untersuchung der Krieferfragmente und Zähne aus dem Grab I, dem Grab II und den Gräbern I und II.[4]

An diesen beiden Ausgrabungen teilnehmen zu dürfen, verdanke ich Dr. Vassos Karageorghis, dem Direktor des Antiquitätendepartements in Cypern und Professor Paul Åström, dem Leiter der schwedischen Cypernexpedition.

UNTERSUCHUNGSMETHODEN

Röntgenologische Untersuchung

Sämtliche Kieferfragmente, die Zähne oder Zahnreste enthielten, wurden einer röntgenologischen Untersuchung unterzogen. Dabei wurde ein Röntgenapparat der Type „RITTER D9", 50 kvs, 10 mA verwendet. Das Filmmaterial bestand aus Kodak DF-58, 3 x 4 cm und 5 x 7 cm. Einer orthoradiellen Einstellung wurde nachgestrebt.

Klinische Untersuchung

Bei zweckmässiger Beleuchtung wurden alle bezahnten Kieferfragmente sowie die einzelnen Zähne und Zahnreste[5] untersucht. Dabei wurde eine dentale Untersuchungssonde der Type „Nordenta 5" verwendet.

Histopathologische Untersuchung

Eine solche Untersuchung ist zeit- und aufwandsmässig sehr umfassend. Das Resultat der Untersuchung, die mo-

---

[1] Betreffs dieses Platzes siehe P. Åström, 'Dromolaxia, Locality "Trypes"', *Report of the Department of Antiquities Cyprus*, 1977, S. 110—112.

[2] Eine vorläufige Erwähnung der Gräber befindet sich im *Annual Report of the Direktor of the Department of Antiquities for the year 1977*, (gedr. 1978), S. 43.

[3] L. & P. Åström *The Swedish Cyprus Expedition*, Vol IV: 1D, Lund 1972, S. 762.

[4] Eine subjektive Schätzung meinerseits ergibt, dass mehr als 2/3 dieses Materials aus dem Grab I kommen.

[5] Nur solche Zahnreste wurden untersucht, bei denen der grösste Teil der Zahnkrone intakt war.

mentan an der histopathologischen Abteilung der zahnärztlichen Hochschule in Göteborg durchgeführt wird, wird später nach Abschluss dieser als komplettierender „Appendix" veröffentlicht.

RESULTAT

Röntgenologische und Klinische Untersuchung

Grab I

Beschreibung des Fundmaterials:

ART	ANZAHL
a) Mandibulafragment mit 3 Zähnen	1
b) Permanente Zähne[6]	19
c) Milchzahn[6]	1

a) Mandibulafragment mit 3 Zähnen (linke Seite):
Röntgen: Allgemeine Scleros im Zahnbereich —
(s. Abb. 1) ein Zeichen für kräftige Kauaktivität. Erweiterter periapikaler Spalt mesiale Wurzel 36[7] — wegen der anomal starken Abrasion ein Zeichen für Pulpairritation.

Klinische
Untersuchung: 35, 36, 37 in situ. Karies 35, 37. Starke Abrasion.
Zahnstein.
Erwachsenes Individuum.

b) Permanente Zähne:
Anzahl 14 + 5 Zahnkeime.[8] Folgende Zähne weisen Veränderungen auf:

GRUPPE[9]	NUMMER[10]	KARIES	MINERALISATIONSDEFEKTE/VERFÄRBUNGEN
INC	1		Gelb
CAN	1		Emailhypoplasie (= E.H.)
	2	x	
PRÄMOL	1		Gelb
	2		Gelb
	3		Gelb, grau
	4		Gelb, grau
MOL	1		Gelb
	2	x	Beige
ZAHNKEIME	1		Beige
	2		Gelb
	3		Braun

c) Milchzahn: Ein Zahn (53?)

Grab II

Beschreibung des Fundmaterials:

ART	ANZAHL
a) Maxillafragment mit 1 Wurzelrest	1
b) Permanente Zähne	9
c) Milchzähne	2

a) Maxillafragment mit 1 Wurzelrest (die Seite konnte nicht eindeutig festgestellt werden).
Röntgen: Keine Anmerkung

Klinische
Untersuchung: ”

b) Permanente Zähne:
Anzahl 9. Folgende Zähne weisen Veränderungen auf:

GRUPPE	NUMMER	KARIES	MINERALISATIONSDEFEKTE/VERFÄRBUNGEN	
INC	1		Gelb	
CAN	1		Braun	
MOL	1		Gelb	Abrasion mit freigelegtem Pulparaum
	2 ←			
	3	x	Beige	
	4		Gelb	

c) Milchzähne: 2 Zähne (53? und 73?) ohne Anmerkungen.

---

[6] R.C. Wheeler, *An Atlas of Tooth Form*, 3:rd edition, London 1962.
[7] Die Nummerierung der Zähne folgt folgendem Schema (vom Betrachter aus von links nach rechts gesehen).

Permanente Zähne
Oberkiefer:

18, 17, 16, 15, 14, 13, 12, 11   21, 22, 23, 24, 25, 26, 27, 28

Unterkiefer:

48, 47, 46, 45, 44, 43, 42, 41   31, 32, 33, 34, 35, 36, 37, 38

Milchzähne
Oberkiefer: 55, 54, 53, 52, 51   61, 62, 63, 64, 65

Unterkiefer: 85, 84, 83, 82, 81   71, 72, 73, 74, 75

[8] Als Zahnkeime werden alle unvollständig entwickelten Zähne bezeichnet.
[9] Vier Zahngruppen gibt es:
Incisive, Canine, Prämolare, Molare. Die Zähne, die nicht genau klassifiziert werden konnten, wurden in diese vier Gruppen eingeordnet.
[10] Alle Zähne, die Veränderungen aufweisen, werden innerhalb ihrer Gruppe nummeriert.

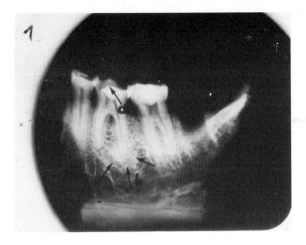

Abb. 1. a) Abrasion, b) Scleros.

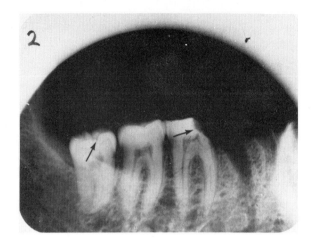

Abb. 2. Kariesschäden.

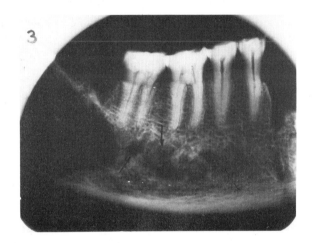

Abb. 3. Radiolucente Gebiete, ev. post mortem.
Osteomyelitis?

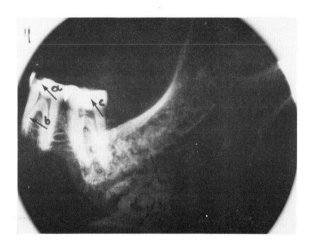

Abb. 4. a) Abrasion, b) Obliteration, c) Karies, d) Scleros,
Etiologie? Osteomyelitis?

Gräber I und II:

Beschreibung des Fundmaterials:

ART	ANZAHL
a) Mandibulafragmente	9
No 1 mit 3 Zähnen	
2 ” 5 ”	
3 ” . 2 ”	
4 ” 6 ” + 1 Wurzelrest	
5 ” 1 Zahn	
6 ” 2 Wurzelresten	
7 ” 1 Zahn	
8 ” 2 Wurzelresten	
9 ” 1 Wurzelrest	
b) Maxillafragment mit 2 Zahnkeimen (No 10)	1
c) Permanente Zähne	107
d) Milchzähne	13
(e) Zahnlose Kieferfragmente	13)

a) Mandibulafragment
   No 1 (rechte Seite)
   Röntgen: Normale Knochenstruktur.

(s.Abb. 2)   Karies: 48, 46.
              Wurzelfraktur 46: post mortem.

Klinische
Unter-
suchung: 48, 47, 46 in situ. Starke Abrasion. Zahn-
              stein.
              Karies 48, 46. Erwachsenes Individuum.

No 2 (rechte Seite)
Röntgen: Radiolucente Gebiete Regio canalis sub-
(s.Abb. 3)   mandibularis — Etiologie? Äussere, post
              mortem — Einflüsse können vermutet
              werden. Osteomyclitis?
              Wurzelrest 48 und Corpusfraktur Regio
              43/42 post mortem.

Klinische
Unter-
suchung: 47, 46, 45, 44, 33 in situ. Starke Abrasion.
              Zahnstein. Erwachsenes Individuum.

No 3 (linke Seite)
Röntgen: Scharf abgegrenzte, runde, sclerotische
(s.Abb. 4)   Gebiete im Corpus mandibularis —
             Etiologie? — Eventuelle äussere Einflüs-
             se post mortem. Osteomyelitis?
             Karies 38. Mesiale Wurzel 37: Oblitera-
             tion wegen starker Abrasion.

Klinische
Unter-   38, 37 in situ. Starke Abrasion. Zahn-
suchung: stein.
             Erwachsenes Individuum.

No 4 (rechte Seite)
Röntgen: Scleros zwischen 48/47 — Etiologie?
(s.Abb. 5)   Eventuell eine „Zahnstocherusur."
             Wurzelrest 33 post mortem.

Klinische
Unter-   48, 47, 46, 45, 44, 43 in situ. Karies 48.
suchung   Starke Abrasion. Zahnstein. Emailhypo-
             plasie. Erwachsenes Individuum.

No 5 (rechte Seite)
Röntgen: Radiopacität regio 47. 47 fehlt (in vivo).
(s.Abb. 6)   Extraktionsalveol 48 während eines Hei-
             lungsprozesses.

Klinische
Unter-   Regio 47 zeigt eine reduzierte Höhe des
suchung: Corpus mandibularis auf. Dagegen ist
             die Dicke grösser als normal. Eventuell
             handelt es sich dabei um eine Callusbil-
             dung, die immer während eines Hei-
             lungsprozesses nach einer Fraktur auf-
             tritt.
             Da der Alveol 48 einen Heilungsprozess
             aufweist, beweist dies die Annahme, dass
             48 einige Monate ante mortem verloren
             gegangen ist. 47 verlor dieses Individu-
             um vermutlich zu dem Zeitpunkt, da die
             Mandibula frakturiert worden ist (einige
             Jahre ante mortem). 46 in situ mit Karies
             und Zahnstein.
             Erwachsenes (eventuell älteres) Indivi-
             duum.

No 6 (rechte Seite)
Röntgen: Wurzelreste Regio 45, 44 — verheilt.
(s.Abb. 7)   Wurzelreste Regio 46 — post mortem.
             Die Relation Foramen mentalis und die
             sehr hoch liegenden Alveolen 43, 42 las-
             sen auf paradontal geschädigte Zähne
             schliessen.

Klinische
Unter-   Stark resorbierter Processus alveolaris.
suchung: Regio 45, 44 ist zahnlos und verheilt, was
             bedeutet, dass diese Zähne einige Jahre
             ante mortem verloren gegangen sind.
             Vermutlich handelt es sich hier um ein
             älteres Individuum.

No 7 (rechte Seite)
Röntgen: 48 ist paradontal geschädigt.
(s.Abb. 8)

Klinische
Unter-   48 in situ. Karies. Starke Abrasion. Gelbe
suchung: Fläcken.

No 8 (rechte Seite)
Röntgen: Radiopacität 47 — verheilte Wurzelreste
(s.Abb. 9)   47, 46 gingen in vivo verloren.

Klinische
Unter-   Stark resorbierter Processus alveolaris —
suchung: älteres Individuum.

No 9 (anteriorer Teil)
Röntgen: Wurzelrest 43 — post mortem.
(s.Abb. 10)

Klinische
Unter-   Keine Anmerkung.
suchung:

b) No 10 (Maxillafragment, rechte Seite)
Röntgen: Zahnkeime für 12 und 11 superior der
(s.Abb. 11) leeren Alveolen für 53, 52, 51 belegen.

Klinische
Unter-   Zwei Zahnkeime sichtbar.
suchung: Das Alter dieses Kindes beträgt 3—4
             Jahre.

c) Permanente Zähne:
   Anzahl 90 + 17 Zahnkeime. Folgende Zähne weisen
   Veränderungen auf:

GRUPPE	NUMMER	KARIES	MINERALISA-TIONSDEFEK-TE/VERFÄR-BUNGEN
INC	1		Gelb
	2	x	Gelb
	3		Gelb
	4	x	
	5		Schwarz
	6		E.H.
	7	x	
	8	x	Gelb
CAN	1	x	Gelb
	2		Gelb
	3		Gelb
	4		E.H.
	5		E.H.
	6		E.H., gelb
	7		E.H.
	8		E.H., gelb
	9	x	Gelb
PRÄMOL	1		E.H., gelb
	2		Gelb
	3		Hellbraun — Weiss
	4		E.H.
	5	x	
	6	x	Braun
	7		Gelb
	8		E.H.

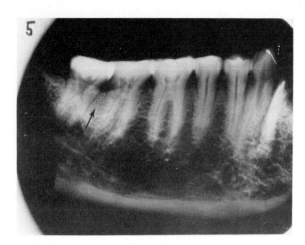

Abb. 5. " Zahnstocherusur".

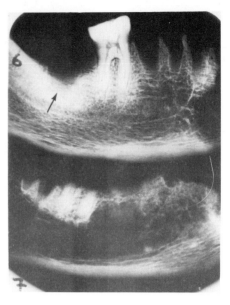

Abb. 6. Heilungsprozess nach dem Verlust von 48, veränderte
Knochenstruktur unter dem Pfeil.
Abb. 7. Wurzelreste 45, 44 — verheilt.

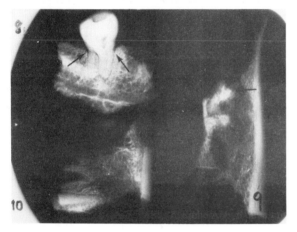

Abb. 8. Paradontale Schäden.
Abb. 9. Wurzelreste 47, 46 — verheilt.
Abb. 10. Wurzelrest 43 — post mortem.

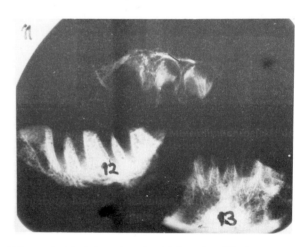

Abb. 11. 2 Zahnkeime eines 3—4 Jahre alten Kindes.
Abb. 12. Zahnloses Mandibulafragment — posteriorer Teil.
Abb. 13. Zahnloses Mandibulafragment — anteriorer Teil.

GRUPPE	NUMMER	KARIES	MINERALISA- TIONSDEFEK- TE/VERFÄR- BUNGEN	
PRÄMOL	9	x	Braun, schwarz	Abra sion mit freigeleg tem Pulpa raum
	10 ←			
	11	x		
MOL (MAXIL-LA)	1		Gelb	
	2		Gelb, schwarz	
	3		E.H.	
	4		E.H.	
	5		E.H.	
MOL (MANDI-BULA)	1		Gelb, schwarz	
	2	x		
	3	x		
	4		Braun	
	5	x		
	6		Gelb	
	7		Braun	
MOL (MAXILLA oder MANDI-BULA)	1		Gelb	
	2		Gelb	
	3		Graubraun	
	4		Gelb	
	5		Gelb	

GRUPPE	NUMMER	KARIES	MINERALISA- TIONSDEFEK- TE/VERFÄR- BUNGEN
ZAHN-KEIME	1		Gelb
	2		Gelb
	3		E.H.
	4		Gelb
	5		Gelb
	6		Graubraun
	7		Schwarz
	8		Gelb
	9		E.H.
	10		Graubraun
	11		Graubraun
	12		Graubraun
	13		Gelb

Peter M. Fischer

d) Milchzäh-
ne: Anzahl 10 + 3 Milchzahnkeime. Da sämtliche Milchzähne identifiziert werden konnten, bekommen sie statt fortlaufender Nummer ihre richtige Zahnnummer.

ZAHNNUMMER	KARIES	MINERALISATIONS-DEFEKTE/VERFÄRBUNGEN
61		
72		
53		
63(Zahnkeim)		Gelb
73		
73		
83(Zahnkeim)		Gelb
54		
74		Gelb, E.H.
55		
75		Gelb
85		Gelb
85(Zahnkeim)		Gelb

DISKUSSION

1) Über das genauere Alter[11, 12] einiger Individuen:

Um das Alter einiger Individuen feststellen zu können, konnten nur die Zahnkeime dafür herangezogen werden. Diese Zahnkeime befanden sich in vivo unter der schützenden Schleimhaut oder auch dem Knochen und waren deswegen äusseren Einflüssen nicht ausgesetzt. Das Alter moderner Individuen wird heute unter anderem mit Hilfe der Abrasion festgestellt. Man kann annehmen, dass diese hier untersuchten Zähne wirklich zum KAUEN verwendet wurden — aus der überaus starken Abrasion zu schliessen —, dass aber auch Verunreinigungen der Speisen — wie z.B. Sand — die Abrasionsstärke beeinflussten. Über die Härte der Speisen oder über den Grad der Verunreinigungen kann jedoch vorläufig nichts Genaueres gesagt werden. Deswegen fällt die Abrasion als Möglichkeit, das Alter feststellen zu können, weg.

Zahnkeime weisen verschiedene Entwicklungsstufen auf. Diese Stufen können ziemlich genau gewissen Altern zugeordnet werden. Das betrifft alle Zahnkeime ausser denen der permanenten Molaren, die eine grössere Variation aufweisen und deswegen hier nicht berücksichtigt werden.

MILCHZAHNKEIME	ALTER (IN JAHREN)
GRÄBER I und II: 63, 83, 85	1,5—2

PERMANENTE ZAHMKEIME		
GRAB I:	CAN	8—10
GRÄBER I und II:	11	5—6
	21	6—8
	31	5—6
	33	13—14
	PRÄMOL	6—8

2) Über die Anzahl der beigesetzten Individuen:

Da Teile der Gräber bei den Schachtarbeiten möglicherweise abgetragen wurden, wird hier die Mindestanzahl der Individuen angegeben.

Grab I:	≥	1 Kind im Alter von 3—6 Jahren
	≥	1 Kind im Alter von 8—10 Jahren
	≥	1 Erwachsener
	≥	3 Individuen

Grab II:	≥	1 Kind im Alter von 3—6 Jahren
	≥	1 Erwachsener
	≥	2 Individuen

Gräber I und II:	≥	1 Kleinkind im Alter von 1,5— 2 Jahren
	≥	4 Kinder im Alter von 1. 3— 4 Jahren 2. 5— 8 Jahren 3. 8—10 Jahren 4. 13—14 Jahren
	≥	7 Erwachsene
	≥	12 Individuen

Ausserdem gab es Tierzähne, die allerdings nicht untersucht wurden.

3) Über die Funktion und Krankheiten der Gebisse:

Die Gebisse wurden wirklich zum Kauen verwendet! Darauf lassen die wohlentwickelten Kiefer und die überaus starke Abrasion schliessen. In 2 Fällen (von allerdings 156) ging die Abrasion sogar soweit, dass der Pulparaum freigelegt wurde. Dies geschieht in moderner Zeit nur ausnahmsweise z.B. bei isolierten Eskimos, die ihre Zähne intensiv benützen. Der freigelegte Pulparaum aber bedeutet, dass diese Individuen Schmerzen gehabt haben müssen. In solchen Fällen tritt eine sogenannte „osteitis periapicalis resorptiva" auf, was „vereiterten Knochen" bedeutet. Die sogenannte „Fokaltheorie" führt ausserdem an, dass andere Teile des Körpers, wie z.B. Herz oder Gelenke, auf Grund dieser Vereiterungen geschädigt werden können.

In 1 Fall kann eine Kieferfraktur mit Zahnverlust vermutet werden. Da diese Fraktur vollkommen verheilt erscheint, muss die Frage gestellt werden: Wie würde dieses befriedigende Resultat erreicht? Heute werden solche Frakturen mit Reposition, Antibiotica, Analgetica und technisch komplizierten Hilfsmitteln, wie z.B. „cap splints", Stahldrähten oder Schrauben behandelt.

In 3 von 11 Kieferfragmenten (27 %), kann von Paradontitis gesprochen werden, was verglichen mit moder-

---

[11] *Pedodonti, Nordisk Lärobok*, Sveriges Tandläkarförbunds Förlagsförening u.p.a., Stockholm 1976, s. 80, Fig. 2, 3.
[12] *Ortodonti, Nordisk Lärobok.* Sveriges Tandläkarförbunds Förlagsförening u.p.a., Stockholm 1971, s. 80, Fig. 8.

nen Gebissen als sehr gering bezeichnet werden muss. 24 von 156 permanenten Zähnen (15 %) weisen Karies auf. Auch diese Ziffer, verglichen mit modernen Zähnen, ist sehr niedrig — die Kariesaktivität also schwach. Gewisse Kariesschäden an atypischen Stellen (z.B. der Aussenseite von Molaren) lassen die Vermutung zu, dass man klebrige Nahrungsmittel genoss, die gerade diese Schäden hervorrufen können. Sämtliche Milchzähne sind kariesfrei.

Emailhypoplasien und Verfärbungen der permanenten Zähne kommen in 73 von 156 Zähnen (47 %) und der Milchzähne in 6 von 16 (38 %) vor. Hier müssen folgende Fragen gestellt werden: Welche Defekte geschahen post mortem? Welche Defekte geschahen im Anschluss an eine allgemeine Erkrankung? War das Wasser stark Fluor-haltig? Falls man die heutigen Fluorwerte für Larnaca studiert, müsste diese letzte Frage mit „Nein" beantwortet werden, da die aktuellen 0,3 ppm (= 0,3 mg/ l)[13] ungefährlich[14] sind und die typischen weiss-gelben Fläcken[15] nicht entstehen lassen können. Da man während der späten Bronzezeit auf Cypern mit einer anderen Vegetation,[16] verglichen mit der heutigen, rechnen muss, kann diese Frage momentan noch nicht beantwortet werden.

Falsche Ernährung — z.B. Mineral — und Vitaminmangel[17] — gibt Anlass zu Mineralisationsdefekten und Emailhypoplasien.

Fieberkrankheiten[18] haben Einfluss auf die Mineralisation der Zähne. Gewisse Nahrungs- und Genussmittel können gelbe, braune und auch schwarze Verfärbungen der Zähne hervorrufen. Eine Aufzählung weiterer Ursachen liesse sich machen.[19]

Die relativ hohe Anzahl der begrabenen Kinder lässt vermuten, dass es sich um eine hohe Kindermortalität handelt. Antworten auf einige der oben gestellten Fragen zu bekommen, hängt von den Resultaten der histopathologischen Untersuchung ab, die noch nicht abgeschlossen ist.

ZUSAMMENFASSUNG

Eine Anzahl Kieferfragmente und Zähne aus zwei Gräbern von Trypes bei Dromolaxia auf Cypern wurden untersucht. Die Gräber gehören der spätcyprischen Bronzezeit an. Der Schwerpunkt der Untersuchung lag in der Registrierung der Karies, Paradontitis, Mineralisationsstörungen und Abrasion. Das Alter und die Anzahl der beigesetzten Individuen wurden, so weit es möglich war, festgestellt.

WÖRTERLISTE mit Erklärungen der im Aufsatz verwendeten Fachwörter

Abrasion	Abnützung
Alveol	Der Kieferteil, der den Zahn beherbergt
Analgetica	Schmerzstillende Heilmittel
Ante mortem	Vor dem Tode
Anterior	Vorderer
Antibiotica	Bakterietötende Heilmittel
Callus	Anschwellung
Canalis submandibularis	Kanal für Unterkiefernerv
Canin	Augenzahn
Cap Splint	Eine Fixierungsbrücke aus Silber
Corpus (mandibularis)	Der grösste Teil des Unterkiefers
Emailhypoplasie	Defekt des Emails
Etiologie	Ursache
Extraction	Herausziehen
Foramen mentalis	Austrittstelle des Unterkiefernervs
Histopathologie	Krankheitslehre mit Hilfe des Mikroskopes
Incisiv	Frontzahn
In situ	An dem richtigen Platz
In vivo	Zu Lebzeiten
Karies	Zahnfäule
Mandibula	Unterkiefer
Maxilla	Oberkiefer
Mesial	Gegen die Mitte
Molar	Backenzahn (einer der hinteren)
Obliteration	Verengung
Orthoradiell	Die Röntgenstrahlen und das Objekt bilden einen 90° Winkel
Osteomyelitis	Knochenmarkinflammation
Paradontitis	Krankheit, die zum Verlust der Zähne führt
Paradontium	Das Gewebe, das den Zahn im Kiefer fixiert
Periapikal	Um die Wurzelspitze herum
Prämolar	Backenzahn (einer der vorderen)
Processus alveolaris	Der Kieferteil, der die Alveolen beherbergt
Post mortem	Nach dem Tode
Pulpa	Zahnnerv
Radiolucent	Strahlen durchlassend (dünner)
Radiopacität	Strahlen auffangend (dichter)
Regio	Gebiet
Reposition	Einrichtung
Resorbtion	Verzehrung
Scleros	Knochenverdichtung
Superior	Oberer
Usur	Zahnabnützung durch frequenten Gebrauch

---

[13] *Studies in Mediterranean Archaeology Vol. XLV:1, Hala Sultan Tekke 1*, Göteborg 1976, S. 110.
[14] *Pedodonti* (supra Anm. 11), S. 174
[15] *Pedodonti* (supra Anm. 11), S. 98, Fig. 52 u. S. 99, Fig. 53, 54.
[16] *Studies in Mediterranean Archaeology Vol. XLV:3, Hala Sultan Tekke 3*, Göteborg 1977, S. 168, 169.
[17] *Pedodonti* (supra Anm. 11), S. 102—104.
[18] *Pedodonti* (supra Anm. 11), S. 102
[19] *Pedodonti* (supra Anm. 11), S. 94, Tabell II.

Abb. 1. A: Plastikmasse, B: Email, C: Dentin, D: Pulpa, E: Wurzel. Die Pfeile markieren 3 kariöse Defekte. 3-fache Vergrösserung.

Abb. 2. A: Emailkaries, B: Intaktes Email, C: Intaktes Dentin. 100-fache Vergrösserung.

APPENDIX

Die histopathologische Untersuchung der Zähne von Trypes.

Einleitung

Diese Untersuchung wurde an der zahnärzlichen Hochschule in Göteborg mit der freundlichen Hilfe von Docent Bengt Magnusson und Zahnarzt Jörgen Norén durchgeführt. Es wurden sowohl intakte als auch kariöse Zähne und solche mit Mineralisationsdefekten und Verfärbungen untersucht.[1]

Methoden[2] und Resultate

Ein Schleifschnitt mit einer Dicke von ca. 100μ wurde angefertigt. Es war leider unmöglich, eine mikroskopische Untersuchung machen zu können, da das Schleifschnittpräparat wegen starker Austrocknung zerfiel.

Eine weitere Methode wurde angewandt, die es unter normalen Umständen möglich macht, die organischen Bestandteile des Dentins[3] untersuchen zu können, — und zwar die Entkalkung eines Schleifschnittpräparates. Auch diese Methode ergab kein untersuchbares Resultat, da nach dem Auslaugen der anorganischen Bestandteile von den organischen Bestandteilen kaum Reste vorhan-

den waren. Auch hier zeigte sich, dass das hohe Alter der Zähne von ca. 3 000 Jahren auf die organischen Bestandteile des Dentins einen zerstörenden Einfluss hatte.

Erst eine dritte Methode erwies sich als erfolgreich. Die zu untersuchenden Zähne wurden in eine Plastikmasse eingebettet. Danach konnten ca. 100μ dicke Schleifschnitte angefertigt werden. Das Resultat der mikroskopischen Untersuchung stimmte mit der klinischen überein: Karies, Mineralisationsdefekte, Emailhypoplasien aber auch Zähne mit vollständiger Mineralisation und ohne andere Defekte wurden festgestellt (siehe Abbildungen).

Von einem ca. 1 mm dicken Schleifschnitt eines — laut klinischer Untersuchung — kariösen Zahnes wurde ein

---

[1] Siehe die Untersuchung der Kieferfragmente und Zähne von Trypes in diesem Teil der *OpAth.*
[2] Gösta Gustafson, *Nordisk Klinisk Odontologi*, band II, Stockholm 1966, 9-I-1—9-I-14.
[3] Dentin besteht aus ca. 30 % organischen und ca. 70 % anorganischen Bestandteilen, Email hingegen aus über 90 % anorganischen Bestandteilen.

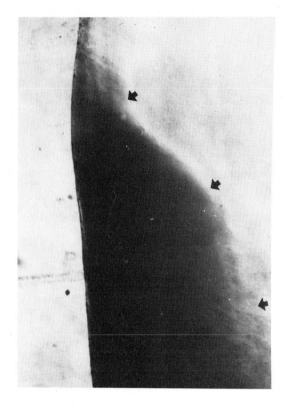

Abb. 3. Emailkaries. 200-fache Vergrösserung.

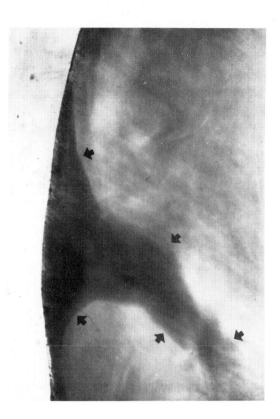

Abb. 4. Emailkaries. 200-fache Vergrösserung.

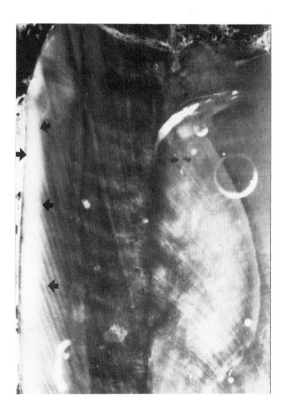

Abb. 5. Mineralisationsdefekte des Emails. 100-fache Vergrösserung.

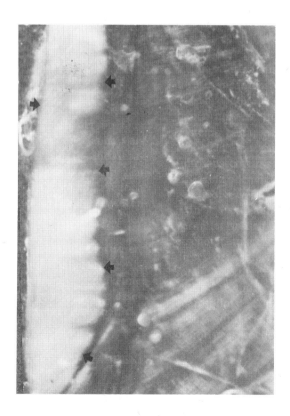

Abb. 6. Mineralisationsdefekte des Emails. 200-fache Vergrösserung.

Peter M. Fischer

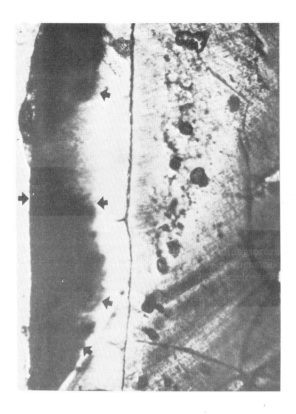

Abb. 7. Siehe Abb. 6 doch mit veränderter Beleuchtung.

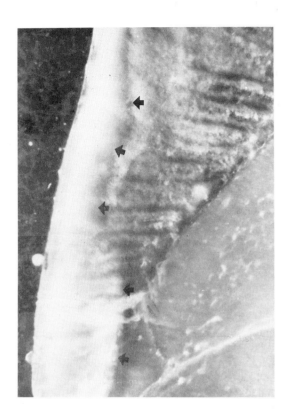

Abb. 8. Mineralisationsdefekte des Emails. 200-fache Vergrösserung.

Mikroradiogramm[4] gemacht. Auch dieses ergab die Diagnose: Karies.

Sämtliche diagnostizierte Defekte unterschieden sich in keiner Weise von Defekten moderner Zähne.

Zusammenfassung

Schleifschnittpräparate von intakten und defekten Zähnen, die in eine Plastikmasse eingebettet worden waren, wurden angefertigt. Die mikroskopische Untersuchung der defekten Zähne ergab folgende Diagnosen: Karies, Mineralisationsdefekte und Emailhypoplasien. Sämtliche Defekte unterschieden sich in keiner Weise von ähnlichen Defekten moderner Zähne. Die intakten Zähne zeigten auch im Mikroskop keine Karies und eine voll-

ständige Mineralisation. Diese Resultate ergaben eine gute Übereinstimmung mit der klinischen Untersuchung.

Schleifschnitte, die nicht zuerst in eine Plastikmasse eingebettet worden waren, zerfielen. Das hohe Alter der Zähne — die ca. 3 000 Jahre — kann als Grund für die Austrocknung der Zähne und für den Zerfall der organischen Bestandteile angenommen werden.

---

[4] Dieses Präparat wurde ca. 60 Minuten schwachen Röntgenstrahlen exponiert.

THE JAWS AND TEETH OF A LATE BRONZE AGE SKELETON FROM HALA SULTAN TEKKE, CYPRUS

INTRODUCTION

In 1979, during the excavations at Hala Sultan Tekke, directed by Professor Paul Åström, a Late Bronze Age shaft grave was discovered. The grave contained one male skeleton.[1] Due to the stratigraphical conditions and the find context the date of this grave is believed to be the middle of the 12th century B.C. The aims of the investigation were:[2]

1. to analyse the dental conditions with respect to caries, periodontal disease and radiographic signs.

2. to examine the dental attrition concerning possible causes and effects and to make a rough age determination.

3. to determine the state of health of the buried individual on the basis of the dental conditions.

MATERIAL AND METHOD

The material consists of the following. One upper jaw fragment (right side) with eight teeth, one upper jaw fragment (left side) with six teeth, one lower jaw fragment (the anterior part) with three teeth, one lower jaw fragment (left side) with three teeth and 10 loose teeth. Some of the teeth are broken and parts of the crowns and roots are missing. The missing teeth are 22 and 31,[3] probably lost *post mortem.*

The investigation was performed by direct inspection and radiographic examination using standardized methods.

RESULTS

1. The dental conditions (Fig. 1–6)

a) Caries: By direct inspection just one tooth can probably be suggested to show caries with an engagement of the pulp: 26. But this is difficult to say with certainty because it is difficult in this case to distinguish between caries *intra vitam* and *post mortem* damage: This tooth has been broken into two parts *post mortem* and a part of it is missing.

The radiographical examination shows only minor *proximal* caries lesions which do not penetrate the enamel.

b) Periodontal disease: An extensive amount of calculus can be observed around all teeth. A combination of calculus, food debris and time resulted in the loss of bone heights, i.e. the loss of tooth bone support. The radiographical examination shows deep proximal bone scores (e.g. see Fig. 6). This individual seems to have suffered a severe degree of periodontal disease.

c) Other radiographic signs: A widening of the periodontal membrane is seen around some roots, due perhaps to increased tooth mobility which can follow periodontal disease.

Other signs observed around some roots are increased radiopacity and increased radioluceny: Pulpal and periodontal diseases could be indicated (see 25, 26 and 27 in Fig. 3). No other pathological finds were observed.

Some teeth (e.g. 45, 35 and 38) show stripes of an intensive radiopaque material inside the pulp chamber. The explanation for this phenomenon perhaps lies in the possible presence of a metallic substance in the soil surrounding the skeleton. There may be a connection with the lilac stain found covering the surface of the jaws and inside bone.

2. Attrition

Attrition is the gradual loss of tooth substance as a result of the chewing of fodd.[4] A considerable occlusal attrition can be seen in this material. The attrition of the molar is shown by means of the highly worn condition of occlusal enamel and by the exposure of large parts of the dentine. Generally speaking, the height of the molar's crown is worn to half. In one case (26) attrition has possibly reached the pulp chamber. The other teeth show a slightly smaller degree of wear.

The wearing down of teeth is a natural process. The increase in attrition due to age proved to be significant.[5] But many external and internal factors have to be considered which make age determination quite uncertain: Abrasive particles in the food acquired by the use of mortar and grinding stones, the chemical and the physical nature of the food influencing the chewing time and the hardness of enamel and dentine. Age determination of skeletal material presents great difficulties.[6] An age determination pattern based on the degree of occlusal attrition can probably increase the reliability of age determination.[7] Using Murphy's index[8] and Sagne's formula[9] the age of the individual is about 31 years. But considering the previously mentioned reservations, this type of age determination is perhaps too speculative. Using Martin's rough group classification[10] the estimated age of this individual is "Adult" (20–40 years) and probably in the upper half.

3. The state of health and habits on the basis of dental conditions

It must be noted that pathological changes in the human body cause discomfort for some individuals but not for others. Therefore only suggestions can be made on which possible pathological changes could influence the state of health.

Just one tooth can probably be suggested to show a caries lesion which in connection with severe attrition could have penetrated the pulp chamber. Such a lesion usually causes pain.

The extensive amount of calculus and the loss of bone heights and the bone scores (i.e. periodontal disease) often cause pus resulting in *halitosis* – bad smelling breath. Usually, periodontal diseases are chronic, bacterial inflammations not giving pain. But theories exist which give periodontal foci of infection a role in systemic diseases (e.g. rheumatic diseases and heart diseases).[11]

It can be assumed that the food eaten by this individual was quite tough requiring powerful chewing. This food together with the use of mortars and grinding stones can be suggested to be the cause of the extensive attrition.

A significant correlation seems to exist between attrition and *temperomandibular* joint (TMJ = jaw joint) arthrosis.[12]

Arthrosis in the TMJ can cause pain especially immediately after waking up.[13] The TMJ feels rigid and painful. The pain lessens when the mandible is moved several times. In some cases it is possible to hear a slight noise from the TMJ during chewing.

Finally it can be said that the jaw bone of the individual is well developed. Exogeneous factors like the powerful chewing required by hard and tough food resulting in well developed chewing muscles may be assumed to be the reason for the vigorous jaws.[14]

CONCLUSIONS

As well as for direct inspection, the use of a radiographical examination of jaws and teeth from an archaeological material seems to be of considerable value. Caries lesions, periodontal disease and pathological changes of the jaw bone can be indicated. Pathological changes of teeth and bone in this archaeological material are not distinguishable from those found in modern material.

In a modern material the dental attrition is an important factor in age determination. But because of a number of unknown – particulary exogenous factors – influencing the dental attrition age determination presents difficulties. A complementary osteological investigation can be valuable.

Conclusions drawn from the dental conditions on the state of health can be seen only as suggestions concerning probable pathological changes in the individual's body eventually causing discomfort. Reliable conclusions on the food eaten by this individual can be drawn from the severe dental attrition: Though, hard and mixed with abrasive particles.

NOTES

1. See the osteological report in *Studies in Mediterranean Archaeology* XLV (Gothenburg) forthcoming.
2. Cf. other dental investigations of Cypriote materials e.g. E. Nyqvist, *Opuscula Atheniensia* XIII, in press, *Levant* XII (1980), 20–21 and *Opuscula Atheniensia* VI (1965), 209.
3. The following teeth nomenclature was used:
   Upper jaw 18, 17, 16, 15, 14, 13, 12, 11, 21, 22, 23, 24, 25, 26, 27, 28.
   Lower jaw 48, 47, 46, 45, 44, 43, 42, 41, 31, 32, 33, 34, 35, 36, 37, 38.
4. M. Klatsky, "Dental Attrition", *Journal of the American Dental Association.* 26, (1939), 73–84.
5. A. E. W. Miles, "Teeth as an Indicator of Age in Man", *Development, Function and Evolution of Teeth* (London–New York–San Francisco 1978), 455–464. G. G. Philippas, "Effects of function on healthy teeth: the evidence of ancient Athenian remains", *J. Am. Dent. Ass.* 45 (1952) 443–453. S. Sagne, "The Jaws and Teeth of a Medieval Population in Southern Sweden", *Ossa* Vol. 3 (Lund 1976), 38–49.
6. S. T. Brooks, "Skeletal Age at Death", *American Journal of Physiology and Anthropology* 13 (1955), 567–597.
7. Sagne (op. cit. in note 4), 16.
8. T. Murphy, "The Changing Pattern of Dentine Exposure in Human Tooth Attrition", *Am. J. Phys. Anthropology* 17 (1959), 167–178.
9. Sagne, (op. cit. in note 4), 46.
10. Martins's group classification:
    1. Infant I 0–7 years, 2. Infant II 7–14, 3. Juvenile 14–20, 4. Adult 20–40, 5. Mature 40–60, 6. Senile 60–. See R. Martin, *Lehrbuch der Anthropologie* (Jena 1928), 580–581.
11. D. F. Mitchell, "The Role of Periodontal Foci of Infection in Systemic Disease", *J. Am. Dent. Ass.* 46 (1953), 32–53.
12. L. E. Bergman and T. Hansson, "Hard Tissue Changes of the Temperomandibular Joint in an Archaeo-Osteological Material from the 11th Century", *Swedish Dental Journal* Vol. 3 (Jönköping 1979), 149–155.
13. R. Wang-Norderud, "Kjeveleddenes Patologi og Terapi", *Nordisk Klinisk Odontologi* IV (Stockholm 1966), 20-V-1.
14. Sagne (op. cit. in note 4), 102.

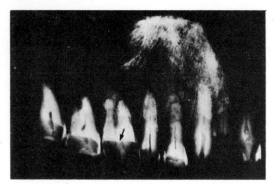

Fig. 1. Upper jaw, right. Severe attrition.

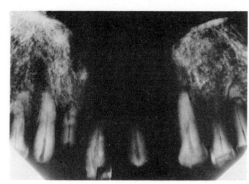

Fig. 2. Upper jaw, front.

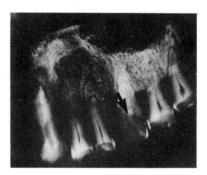

Fig. 3. Upper jaw, left. Possible
caries lesion.

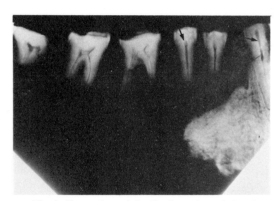

Fig. 4. Lower jaw, right. Radiopacity, etiology?

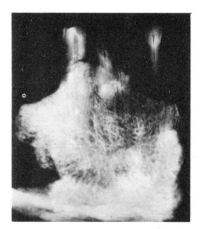

Fig. 5. Lower jaw, front.

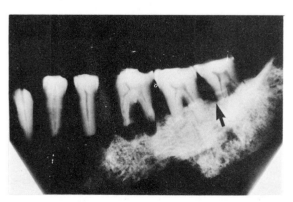

Fig. 6. Lower jaw, left. Bone score (periodontal disease).

RESISTIVITY MEASUREMENTS AT HALA SULTAN TEKKE, CYPRUS

INTRODUCTION

During the campaign at Hala Sultan Tekke in 1972 Ing. R. E. Linington, Lerici Foundation, Rome, carried out a magnetic prospecting using a differential proton magnetometer.[1] Because of difficulties with the proton magnetometer, caused by very hot weather conditions, and the short surveying time available, Ing. Linington recommended electrical prospecting. He did, however, have some reservations concerning the validity of the method in very hot weather and dry soil conditions.

The purpose of the author's electrical prospecting during the campaign at Hala Sultan Tekke in 1979 was:

1. To find out if it is possible to carry out electrical prospecting using a "Geohm" instrument under the hot and very dry summertime conditions in Cyprus.[2]

2. To compare possible results of the electrical prospecting with those of the magnetic prospecting done in the same area in 1972.

3. To compare possible results of the electrical prospecting with those of succeeding excavations.

4. To try to trace a possible city wall in the western part of the town.

INSTRUMENT AND METHOD[3]

The electrical instrument used was a "Geohm" manufactured by Gossen, West Germany, fed by a storage battery with a life of about 40 hours. The "Geohm" is an instrument giving direct measurements of the V/I ratio according to Ohm's law $R = \frac{V}{I}$ where R is the electrical resistance of the soil, V is the direct current voltage and I the current flowing through the soil. The "Wenner normal system", which measures resistivity by feeding a known electrical current into the ground by means of a pair of electrodes (Fig. 1:1 and 4) and measures the voltage produced across a second pair of electrodes, was used (Fig. 1:2 and 3). The four electrodes were placed in the ground, 1 m apart, thus giving total separation of 3 m. The "x1" scale was used; values below 5 were measured with the "0,1" scale and multiplied by 10 before registering them.[4] The correlation between the instrument reading R, in Ohm and the absolute electric resistivity (ρ) is that $\rho = 6,28 \times R \times 1$ m. This set of four electrodes is moved between readings without changing the dimensions of the four-pole pattern along east – west lines within a grid system. In such a case of horizontal prospecting it is possible that an abnormally high restivity below ground can correspond to archaeological features (e.g. lime stone walls), which should be expected because of results obtained by the proton magnetometer survey and the earlier excavations.

One of the main problems with dry conditions is to achieve sufficient contact between the electrodes and the soil. Iron rods with a diameter of 2 cm and a length of 60 cm were chosen for electrodes. Tests were made to find out how deeply the electrodes should be driven in to achieve sufficient contact. It was found that between 10 cm and 30 cm the restivity values tended to fall, and between 30 cm and 50 cm the restivity values remained constant. As a result, 40 cm was considered to give sufficient contact and was used during the whole investigation. This type of electrical prospecting is strenous work and in order to speed it up, and to save man power, five electrodes were used and four assistants worked simultaneously (Fig. 1).

Assistant A: Reads the instrument (G)
      "   B: Changes the pole clamps (a–d)
      "   C: Drives the electrodes in (1–5)
      "   D: Pulls the electrodes out (1–5)

RESULTS FROM AREA 8 SOUTH

1. The grid system (see the map on p. 40 and see Fig. 2)

In order to compare possible results of the electrical prospecting with those of the magnetic prospecting, Area 8 South (30 m x 20 m) lying to the south of Area 8 and to the north of Area 21 was surveyed. A close connection between the already excavated Area 8 and the new Area 8 South was achieved by an east – west survey line of 20 m (FFi/FFk). It was not possible to survey the remaining 10 m due to a small land-slide.

2. Method of representation used

Electrical prospecting can make it possible to trace stone constructions. The method of representation used in this investigation is that of a symbol diagram. The different symbols are chosen to point out what seem to be interesting structures. The same symbols, which Ing. Linington used in his magnetic investigation in 1972,[5] were chosen to make a direct comparison possible (Fig. 3):

Electrical survey: (blank)   −3,3
(Fig. 3 A)   (·)   3,4–4,4
                     (O)   4,5–5,5
                     (●)   5,6–6,6
                     (●)   6,7–

Magnetic survey: (blank) 7–
(Fig. 3 B)   (·)   2–6
                    (O)   −3–1
                    (●)   −8--4
                    (●)   −13--9

The choice of upper and lower limits with respect to each symbol was based on the following facts: There appears to be a definite step between the group of values 4,1 to 5,7 and the group 2,2 to 3,3. The examples below illustrate this (see Fig. 2):

FFk/FGa 506/507 = 4,1/3,3
FGe/FGf 504/505 = 4,8/2,9
FGk/FHa 501/502 = 5,0/3,3
FHi/FHk 496/497 = 5,7/2,2

On the assumption that these values show the difference between architectural remains and the absence of architectural remains, two different symbols were chosen. The choice of 3,3 (blank) and 3,4 (·) is quite subjective. This transition could be set some decimals higher or lower, of course. The fact that the values between c. 3,0 and down to 1,2 tended to fall without any definite steps, strengthens the hypothesis mentioned above. There seems to be a further step between high values (●) and very high values (●).
The examples below illustrate this:

FGk/FHa 495–498 = 6,2/7,0/7,1/7,0/6,0
FGa/FGb 483–490 = 6,5/7,1/7,0/6,4/7,4/
                   6,1/6,8/6,4
FGf/FGg 496–503 = 6,1/6,8/5,8/7,6/7,2/
                   7,1/7,2/6,0

Here again the choice of − 6,6 (●) and 6,7 − (●) is subjective and can be set some decimals higher or lower.

The average value of all the 620 values is approximately 4,5 (exactly 4,4579). In the symbol diagram the average value is c. 5,0 due to a mathematical distribution of the values between 3,3 and 6,7 which means that the symbols., O,● enclosed 11 decimals each. The excavations during the campaigns in 1972 in Area 21[6] and 1972–1978 in Area 8[7] resulted in the exposure of primarily architectural remains. The results of the excavations in Area 8 and Area 21 can be said to be the reason that Area 8 South contains primarily architectural remains.

3. Interpretation of the results
The south-east triangle (Fig. 4 A):
The symbol diagram appears to confirm the hypothesis of two types of anomalies: There appears to exist a distinct border line running from the north-east corner in a south-west direction that distinguishes an area of possible stone constructions from an area without architecture. The area without architecture may be a courtyard, a roadway or simply an open space outside a building. Another possibility is destruction due to ploughing since the original architecture lay on a higher level in ancient times.

The south-west triangle (Fig. 4 B):
This quite irregular pattern of possible stone constructions could be an area of destroyed architecture.

The pentagonal area (Fig. 4 C):
This pentagon seems to consist of a number of a heavy stone constructions. The more regular pattern of this area has the appearance of walls forming rooms and surrounding courtyards. Even though a detailed interpretation is quite difficult, and full of uncertainties, an experimental interpretation is shown in Figure 5A. The results of previous excavations in area 8 and Area 21 have been taken into account when making this interpretation. Areas of possible architecture are indicated by diagonal lines. Where it has been possible to determine the course of separate walls, a continuous line has been used. Probable walls are indicated by broken lines.

COMPARISON WITH THE MAGNETIC RESULTS

A direct comparison can be made in Figure 3. The use of two different orientations of the grid system resulted in slight deviations of the north-south and east-west lines.[8]

The south-east triangle (fig. 4 A):
Very good agreement exists between both investigations in zone A1. Zone A2 shows a different interpretation: No architectural remains are assumed in the electrical investigation while the magnetic results suggest a possible continuation in A2 of a substantial construction[9] beginning in zone C5.

The south-west triangle (Fig. 4 B):
In the northern zone B1 the electrical investigation suggests remains of stone constructions while the magnetic suggests no architectural remains. In the southern zone B2, a difference in interpretation also

exists: The electrical investigation assumes remains of stone constructions, the magnetic suggests more substantial constructions.

The pentagonal area (Fig. 4 C):
The greatest difference between the two investigations is found in zone C1 and C3. While the electrical interpretation suggests substantial stone constructions, the magnetic suggests no constructions at all. On the other hand there is excellent agreement between the two investigations in the zones C2 and C4–C8 which represent the largest part. Both investigations suggest stone constructions.

A new experimental interpretation of the magnetic results is made by the author in Figure 6. The results of the previous excavations in Area 8 and Area 21 have been taken into account when making this interpretation, resulting in a more detailed one than that made by Ing. Linington in 1972. Areas of possible architecture are indicated by diagonal lines and probable architecture by broken lines.

COMPARISON WITH THE EXCAVATION RESULTS (FIG. 5 A, B)

At the end of the 1980 campaign the excavations of Area 8 South had proceeded so far as to give a basis for a comparison with the experimental interpretation.

The distinct border between C and A as illustrated in the schematic diagram (Fig. 4) and interpretation (Fig. 5 A) is believed also to exist (see the long wall that separates C4, C5, C6 and A1, A2 in Fig. 5 B). This wall seems to represent a border line delineating an area with stone construction from an area without architecture (A).

In the south-west triangle (Fig. 4 B) some walls – partly shown in Figures A – a street, a ditch and heaps of stone were excavated.

The pentagonal area C has shown the continuation of the previously excavated room-complex from Area 8: A number of rooms with courtyards enclosed by partly, well built walls of varying widths that form an orthogonal pattern. Some walls have collapsed, however, the more well-built and stable walls still remain.

Even though, in the experimental interpretation from Figures 5 A, it was impossible to include the courses of all the walls, it has been possible with the good agreement of excavation results, to include the more substantial walls and to show areas with stone constructions and an area without architecture.

THE SEARCH FOR THE CITY WALL

In agreement with M. Fortin's hypothesis about the localization of the city wall[10] parts of two grids were investigated with the "Geohm": E3 and G2/G3. The geographical conditions present prompted the search for the town's defensive wall in these particular areas. An excellent place for the town's defence is e.g. the high plateau in E3 surrounded by a very steep slope in the north and west. Another place is the plain sloping to the west between the hill in G2 and a well in G3.

Due to shortage of time no further investigations could be performed.

GRID E3

The size of the investigated area in E3 is about 1,200 m². A horizontal prospecting has been performed along lines measuring between 15 m and 33 m. These lines pointed in a nearly north-south direction and the distance between them was 3 m. The same pole pattern as in the previous investigation was used.

The instrument readings ranged from 2.7 to 22.9 (scale x1). Test trenches were dug, in areas with very low values (around 3.0), in areas with average values (around 12.0), and in areas with very high values (around 20.0). In these areas sherds were found only in the surface layer. In deeper layers no sherds or architectural remains were discovered. The low values corresponded to loose and sandy soils, the average values to loose and sandy soils mixed with small pebbles, and the high values to compact limestone.

GRIDS G2/G3

The lines, between a well east of Area 23 in G3 and the foot of the hill in G2, were investigated. These lines pointed in a nearly east-west direction and the same prospecting and pole pattern as in E3 was used.

The instrument readings ranged from 1.6 to 33.5 (scale x1). Just one value turned out to be as high as 33.5, which corresponded to solid rock shown by a test trench. The highest value next to 33.5 was 18.5. Other test trenches were dug in areas with low values (around 3.0), in areas with average values (around 7.0), and in areas with high values (around 15.0). As previously mentioned sherds were found only in the surface layer here too. The number of sherds was higher in this area. No architectural remains or sherds were discovered in deeper layers. The results from the test trenches turned out to be comparable to E3: Low values corresponded to loose and sandy soils, average values to loose and sandy soils mixed with small pebbles, and high values to compact limestone.

That the city wall has not been found may be because its stone may have been used to build the nearby mosque or used by the local inhabitants for house building. Certain reservations must, however, be made to this interpretation as the investigated area was so small. It is also possible that the course of the city wall is different from that previously thought, e.g. that the course of the wall passes in a northerly direction through Area 23, directly towards the high plateau, where Area 6 is situated. Supplementary measurements could be of value.

GENERAL CONCLUSIONS

Resistivity measurements with a "Geohm" instrument are time-consuming and arduous, however, apart from the fact that four assistants are needed to carry out the prospecting, the method is very cheap to use.

The results, compared to the succeeding excavations, have been satisfying. The use of heavy electrodes, hammered down to a depth of 40 cm, gave clearly measurable and interpretable values which made electrical prospecting at Hala Sultan Tekke possible. The very warm and dry climatic conditions in Cyprus in the summertime have not hindered electrical prospecting. The stable weather conditions in Cyprus during summer – rain being very rare – and stable soil humidity can be considered advantageous for electrical prospecting. Electrical prospecting usually demands many days work. Because of the above mentioned stable soil humidity, the results of different days can be compared with each other, without having to take into consideration the daily varying humidity values. The excavation results, up to now, generally confirm the experimental interpretation based on electrical prospecting. With electrical prospecting it seems to be possible to obtain a more detailed interpretation than that obtained by magnet-

ic prospecting, at least under the conditions at Hala Sultan Tekke (cf. Fig. 5 A and Fig. 6).

Because of the slower pace of electrical prospecting it is more practical to use magnetic prospecting for a large scale survey. However, when Hala Sultan Tekke is considered, the 1972 proton magnetometer survey has already charted a large area and shown areas of architectural remains and "empty" spaces. An electrical prospecting of especially interesting areas and of areas which consist of dubious magnetic anomalies.[11] is consequently of considerable value.

NOTES

1. R. E. Linington, *Studies in Mediterranean Archaeology* Vol. XLV Hala Sultan Tekke 3 (Gothenburg 1977), 13–27.
2. Other electrical resistivity surveys were performed by the French expedition at Amathus. See Bulletin de Correspondance Hellénique 103 (1979), 756–762.
3. For further information on different instruments and methods see M. J. Aitken, "Electrical Resistivity Surveying", *Physics and Archaeology* (Oxford 1974), 267–286. R. J. C. Atkinson, "Resistivity Surveying in Archaeology", *The Scientist and Archaeology* (London 1963), 1–30, E. W. Carpenter, "Some Notes concerning the Wenner Configuration", *Geophysical Prospecting 3* (1955), 388–402, M. S. Tite, *Methods of Physical Examination in Archaeology*, Seminar Press (London–New York 1972), 47–52.
4. See "Geohm-Messanleitung", "Geohm's" instructionsbook.
5. Linington, op. cit. (in note 1), 20, Fig. 8, 21.
6. B. Frizell, op. cit. (in note 1), 30–57.
7. G. Hult, op. cit. (in note 1), 58–91 and Vol. XLV:4 (Gothenburg 1978) 1–94. The excavations during 1976–1978 are not yet published.
8. Linington, op. cit. (in note 1), 19.
9. Linington, op. cit. (in note 1), 25–26.
10. See M. Fortin's hypothesis about the localization of the city wall in his Ph. D. thesis on the Military Architecture of Cyprus during the Second Millennium B. C. to be presented at the University of London.
11. Cf. Linington, op. cit. (in note 1), 26.

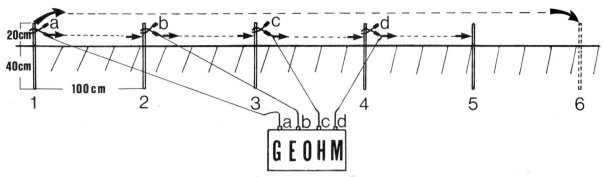

Fig. 1. The "Geohm" and the "Wenner normal system".

Readings and pole patterns:

1st	1a, 2b, 3c, 4d
2nd	2a, 3b, 4c, 5d
3rd	3a, 4b, 5c, 1d
4th	4a, 5b, 1c, 2d
5th	5a, 1b, 2c, 3d

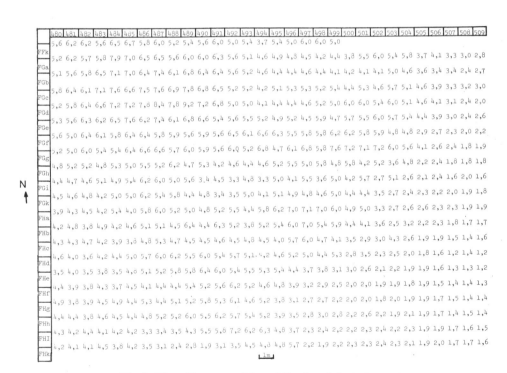

Fig. 2. The grid system of Area 8 South and the instrument
readings.

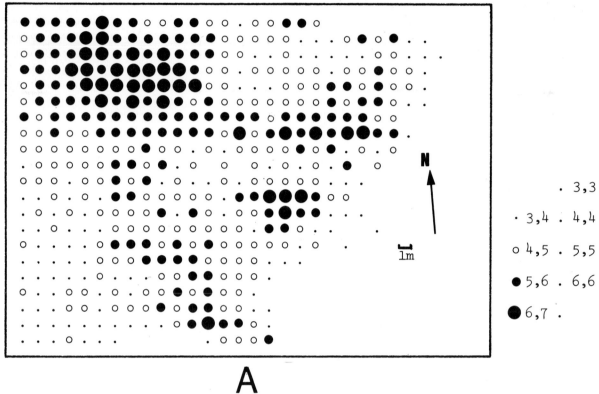

A

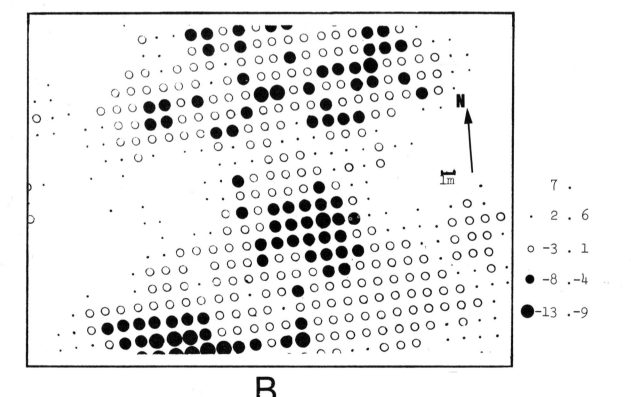

B

Fig. 3. A: Symbol diagram of the electrical prospecting.
B: Symbol diagram of the magnetic prospecting.

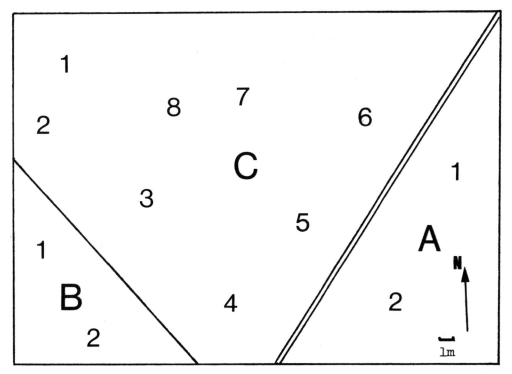

Fig. 4. Schematic diagram of Area 8 South based on the interpretation of the electrical results.

26

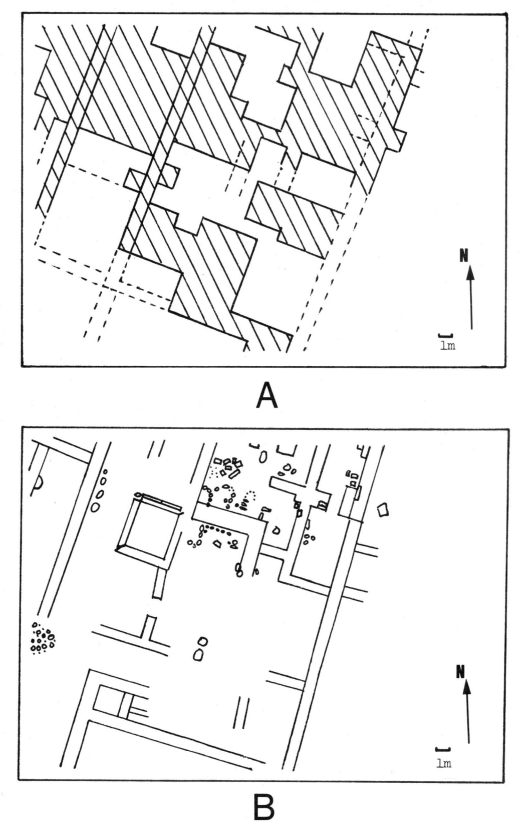

A

B

Fig. 5. A: An experimental interpretation of the electrical results.
Fig. 5. B: An approximate sketch of the excavation results (August 1980).

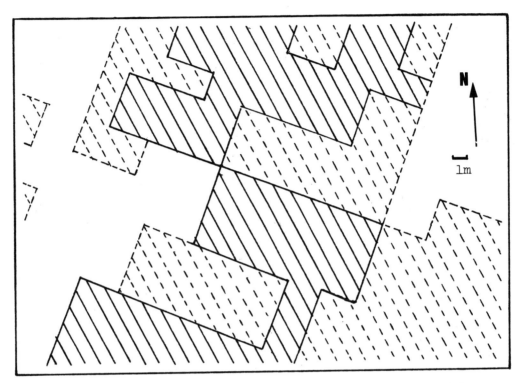

Fig. 6. A revised experimental interpretation of the magnetic results obtained in 1972.

ISBN 91-85086-34-7

THE USE OF A METAL DETECTOR IN ARCHAEOLOGY

BY

PETER M. FISCHER

During the excavations at Hala Sultan Tekke in 1978, the Swedish Cyprus expedition, directed by Professor Paul Åström, used a C-Scope TR 400/500 metal detector made in Great Britain by Candle-International Ltd, Ashford, Kent. The detector consists of a waterproof, isocon, search head and an instrument which registers metal finds (Fig. 1). The instument consists of the following parts (Fig. 2):

A. Contact for headphones.
B. On/Off button; fine adjustment.
C. Rough adjustment.
D. Loudspeaker.
E. Battery control (two batteries of type PP6 9V are used, which last for about 40 hours).
F. Indicating instrument.

To adjust the instrument so that it works properly, the following procedure must be followed.

Turn on B and then turn on C until a high-pitched sound is heard from the loudspeaker. Turn B back until the sound is just about to disappear. If the basic sound is too high or quite inaudible, the sensitivity of the instrument is decreased.

The distance between the search head and the examined surface has to be about 3—4 cm. Furthermore, the search head and the surface must be parallel.

Results

A large area in the central part of the Late Bronze Age town of Hala Sultan Tekke was cleared of surface soil with a bull-dozer. In the field east of Area 8, the instrument gave no indication of metal finds when the scraped soil was searched. In three places where loose soil was still present, the detector indicated two tin cans and one capsule, all three about 5 cm below the surface. It was not practical to use the instrument over loose and uneven soil, as it gave too many wrong indications of cavities.

A treasure containing 15 pieces of gold, one piece of bronze and seven pieces of faience and precious stones was found in Area 8 East. The objects were later placed on a stone floor and tested individually with the instrument, which gave no indication of a thin, 5-mm-wide sheet of gold and a small bronze pin but indicated the thin, slightly larger pieces of gold and the other, larger ones, 15 pieces in all. After the treasure was found, the instument indicated an iron object about 10 cm away from the treasure. In the same area, measuring about 500 m², more finds were detected with the instrument.

---

[1] See the excavation report in *Studies in Mediterranean Archaeology* Vol. XLV, forthcoming.

Area 8 East:

Find No.[1]	Object	Material	Size before cleaning, cm	Excavated depth, cm
N 1159 (Fig. 3)	Round piece	Iron	3.1x2.3	10
N 1171 (Fig. 4)	Net weight	Lead	2.3x1.6	3
N 1172 (Fig. 5D)	Sling bullet	Lead	3.7x1.7	8
N 1173 (Fig. 6)	Drop-shaped piece	Lead	1.8x1.5	3
N 1174 (Fig. 7)	Coin	Copper	Ø 1.9	1
N 1178 (Fig. 8)	Rectangular piece	Lead	3.8x2.4	8
N 1179 (Fig. 9)	Oval piece	Lead	2.0x1.5	4
N 1180 (Fig. 10)	Triangular piece	Bronze	3.2x2.8	3

Fig. 1. The author using the detector.

Fig. 2. The instrument.

Fig. 3. Iron piece.

Fig. 4. Lead net weight.

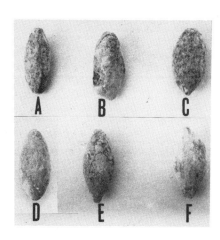

Fig. 5. Lead sling bullets.
A: N 1161, B: N 1166, C: N 1167*a*,
D: N 1172, E: N 6091, F: N 6093.

Fig. 6. Lead piece.

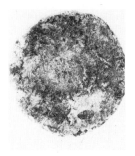

Fig. 7. Copper coin.

Fig. 9. Lead piece.

Fig. 8. Lead piece.

Fig. 10. Bronze piece.

The other areas already excavated or under excavation were also investigated with the detector.

In Area 22, measuring about 600 m², the instrument gave a strong indication of two lead sling bullets.

Area 22:

Find No.	Object	Material	Size, cm	Excavated depth, cm
N 6091 (Fig. 5E)	Sling bullet	Lead	3.7x1.6	5
N 6093 (Fig. 5F)	Sling bullet	Lead	3.7x1.7	3

In Area 8, measuring about 450 m², 13 objects were located with the detector. They consisted of four lead sling bullets, one lead weight, one bronze knife, one net weight, and bronze fragments. In the same area, at a place where the excavations were already finished, the most interesting of all the finds a 40-cm, lead string was found underneath a 9-cm-thick (!), limestone plaque on the floor of a bathroom. A lead sling bullet and a lead, net weight were also discovered underneath a limestone plaque about 8 cm thick (!).

Area 8:

Find No.	Object	Material	Size, cm	Excavated depth, cm
N 1160 (Fig. 11, 12)	Round weight	Lead	Ø 5.3x1.8	10
N 1161 (Fig. 5A)	Sling bullet	Lead	3.5x1.4	3
N 1162 (Fig. 13)	Knife	Bronze	18.8x2.0	2
N 1163 (Fig. 14)	Rectangular piece	Bronze	6.6x3.0	5
N 1164 (Fig. 15)	Rectangular piece	Bronze	3.3x1.4	On surface
N 1165 (Fig. 16)	Triangular piece	Bronze	4.8x1.9	8
N 1166 (Fig. 5B)	Sling bullet	Lead	3.5x1.6	5
N 1167 a (Fig. 5C)	Sling bullet	Lead	3.5x1.8	Underneath 8-cm-thick lime stone plaque
N 1167 b (Fig. 17)	Two net weights	Lead	4.8x1.3	Underneath 8-cm-thick lime stone plaque
N 1168 (Fig. 18)	String	Lead	c. 40.0x5.0	Underneath 9-cm-thick lime stone plaque
N 1169 (Fig. 19)	Rectangular piece	Bronze	3.6x3.0	5
N 1170 (Fig. 20)	Seven fragments	Bronze	3.8x3.6	8
			3.5x1.8	
			3.2x3.0	
			1.7x1.2	
			1.2x0.9	
			1.0x0.7	
			0.7x0.5	

The detector also indicated chalky limestone, both in blocks and in crushed form. It is useful to know that walls of chalky limestone may be discovered by the instrument underneath the surface. The sound indicating metal is much better defined and louder than that indicating chalky limestone, which makes it possible to distinguish signals for metal finds and limestone.

In order to detect the metal objects underneath stones, it was necessary to reduce the electrical power with buttons B and C (Fig. 2).

Furthermore, it is also possible to detect cavities under surface soils. The signal for cavities is much less significant than that for metals and less significant than the signal indicating chalky limestone. The explanation of the changed signals lies in the fact that the resistance in this "disturbed" soil beneath the search head is different

Fig. 11. Lead weight *in situ*.

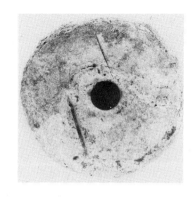

Fig. 12. Lead weight.

Fig. 14. Bronze piece.

Fig. 15. Bronze piece.

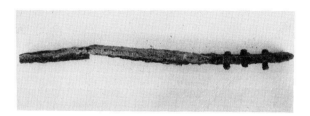

Fig. 13. Bronze knife.

Fig. 16. Bronze piece.

Fig. 18. Lead string *in situ*.

Fig. 17. Lead net weight.

Fig. 19. Bronze piece.

Fig. 20. Bronze fragments.

from that in compact soil. The instrument does not register copper slag or very corroded pieces of metal which contain almost only metal oxides.

Discussion

A metal detector is an excellent aid in field archaeology. Pieces of metal with a crust of oxides and much earth adhering to them are difficult to detect and may be assumed to be stones or daubs. For example, during the 10 days the detector was in action, it detected six sling bullets, which is more than were ever found before in a single season between 1972 and 1977 at Hala Sultan Tekke.[2]

The lead string from Area 8, which perhaps served as a sealing material between the limestone plaques, would probably never have been found without the detector. In some cases, even though the instrument gave a signal for the presence of a metal object and therefore it was natural to expect one it was difficult and sometimes impossible to find the object without further help from the detector.

A metal detector provides an insurance that no metal objects will be missed, except for the very small and thin ones.

The smallest object found by the detector was a bronze fragment about 0.5 cm^2 large.

It is strongly recommended that all excavations should be concluded by testing the excavated surface with the detector.

Summary

During the campaign in 1978 at Hala Sultan Tekke, the Swedish Cyprus expedition used the C-Scope TR 400/500 metal detector. The detector tested an area of about 2 000 m^2 and indicated 22 metal objects between 40.0 x 5.0 cm and 0.7 x 0.5 cm in size. It indicated the presence of bronze, copper, gold, iron and lead. The finds were located both "on the surface" and down to 10 cm beneath the surface.[3]

The detector even revealed the presence of limestone in blocks and in crushed form and cavities were also indicated.

---

[2] See the paper on lead sling bullets by Paul Åström and Ino Nicolaou in this volume of *OpAth.*.

[3] Wakebo, the engineering firm which distributes C-Scope detectors in Sweden declares that a Swedish crown (Ø 2.5 cm) can be detected down to 25—30 cm beneath the surface and a metal box down to c. 75 cm.

REPORTS FROM THE FIELD
GEOPHYSICAL PROSPECTING AT HALA SULTAN TEKKE, CYPRUS

During the 1979 season of excavation of the Late Cypriot Bronze Age town at Hala Sultan Tekke, the writer carried out an electro-magnetic survey with the help of a Very Low Frequency Discriminative Detector (VLF-Discriminator). The survey resulted in the discovery of a rich shaft grave and in an area of some 10,000 sq. m., 159 metal artifacts (bronze, copper, gold, iron, lead and silver) as well as some non-metal objects and features. Comparisons were made with two other electro-magnetic devices, a Pulsed Induction (PIM) and an Induction Balance (IB) detector. The tests favoured the VLF detector. The results of a resistivity survey also were compared with those from the proton magnetometer survey made in 1972 and with the findings of subsequent excavation. The agreement between the two surveys and the subsequent excavation was good.

THE ELECTRO-MAGNETIC SURVEY

Introduction

During the 1979 excavations by the Swedish Cyprus Expedition at Hala Sultan Tekke (see map. Fig. 1), directed by Professor Paul Åström, two electro-magnetic detectors were used by the author: a Very Low Frequency Discriminative detector (VLF-Discriminator),[1] C-Scope VLF 1000, made by Candle International Ltd, Ashford, Kent, England, and a Pulsed Induction detector (PIM) ELSEC 900, made by Littlemore Scientific Engineering Company, Oxford, England (Fig. 2).

The purposes of the survey were:

1. to discover possible advantages/disadvantages as compared with the Induction Balance "wide scan" detector (IB), C-Scope TR 400/500, used by the author at the same site in 1978;[2]

2. to discover possible advantages/disadvantages of the VLF/PIM detectors by systematic usage throughout the excavation;

3. to perform a surface survey for the purpose of indicating and thereafter excavating possible finds from the surface layer, thereby anticipating and discouraging the illegal use of detectors in the vicinity of the present excavation;

4. to test the possibility of discovering non-metal objects and features via the VLF detector.[3]

Results

1. In order to check the survey made by the IB detector in 1978, the site was examined once more, this time with the VLF/PIM detectors. No excavation has been undertaken on the site since 1978. In view of the fact that the VLF/PIM detectors indicated more metal finds they may be adjudged superior to the IB detector.

2. The VLF detector was used during the excavation of the central section of the town (approximately 600 sq. m.), layer by layer. The PIM detector was only sporadically used. The decision to abstain from continual recourse to the PIM detector was prompted by an empirical finding; the search could not be pursued with both detectors simultaneously. The pulse emitted by the PIM detector disturbed the operation of the VLF detector if the two devices were used simultaneously within 10 m of each other. This inconvenience gave rise to tests to determine which device was to be preferred. The tests favoured the VLF detector because it provided faster indication, greater sensitivity to small objects, more precise fixes, lower power consumption (the batteries last for 30–40 hours), and an opportunity to assess the value of a VLF-Discriminator which, according to the manufacturer, can differentiate between metals before the objects are brought to light. During the survey, tests verified these claims, provided the device is used in the three discriminate modes (D1, D2, and D3). The normal mode (N) gave the highest sensitivity and greatest depth penetration, and the instrument indicated both ferrous and non-ferrous metal objects. The discriminate mode D1 did not respond to iron, D2 rejected iron and silver paper, and D3 did not respond to iron, ferrous alloys, and silver paper. A minor disadvantage of the VLF compared with the PIM detector is that the former is more complicated to use. The user must practice with the instrument for several weeks in order to achieve maximum proficiency in all modes.

The layer-by-layer survey resulted in the discovery of 101 metal artifacts (Table 1). Some finds and find circumstances will be described in greater detail in order to demonstrate the advantages of a sophisticated electro-magnetic instrument.

In an area where the excavations were finished for this season, a check with the VLF detector gave unusually strong indications of metal. The readings persisted in the discriminate mode D3 over an area of some 2 sq. m., which signified large, non-ferrous objects. New excavations brought to light an intact, rich, shaft grave at a depth of about 60 cm., containing *inter alia* three bronze vessels, a gold necklace with a scarab and cartouche, a gold finger ring, a bronze dagger, three bronze arrowheads, a bronze bolt, a piece of silver, and a bronze trident (Figs. 3, 4).

During the survey, 21 lead sling bullets, which are extremely difficult and sometimes impossible to distinguish from stones, were discovered (Figs. 5, 6). Lead sling bullets are of special interest because they sometimes carry inscriptions in Cypro-Minoan, an as yet undeciphered script.[4] The instrument indicated the presence and the extent of somewhat brittle metal artifacts, e.g., a bronze spearhead (Fig. 7). A bronze bracelet which lay buried beneath a stone slab (Fig. 8) and a small gold bead enclosed in daub were distinctly located by the VLF detector (Fig. 9).

3. A surface survey was executed over c. 10,000 sq. m. surrounding the present excavation area; metal artifacts were discovered (see Table 1). One interesting discovery in the surface layer was the presence of 11 lead sling bullets which presumably derived from a deeper layer. Their proximity to the surface is perhaps a result of the use of modern deep-ploughing bulldozers in these areas. On the other hand, these areas may have been at a higher level in ancient times, and thereby more exposed to the devastating effects of ploughing. Other intriguing finds were two 750 g lead weights (Fig. 10).

4. The possibility was revealed of discovering non-metal objects with the aid of the VLF detector. Whole vessels, substantial sherds, concentrations of sherds in a limited area, compact pieces of terracotta, mud bricks, hornblende (a mineral containing aluminium, iron, magnesium, calcium and usually sedium), and chalky limestone were indicated. Changes in soil type and structure obviously enable the VLF detector to distinguish between different archaeological layers and features and ash. The instrument readings indicative of non-metal objects and features diverge from those received from metal artifacts.

THE RESISTIVITY SURVEY

The purpose of this survey was to discover whether or not it is feasible to carry out electrical prospecting at Hala Sultan Tekke,[5] and to compare possible results with the proton magnetometer survey of the same area in 1972, as well as with the results of subsequent excavations. It was also hoped that the survey would help to trace the northern and western stretches of the town wall.

The survey was performed via a standard Geohm instrument and 60 cm electrodes (D = 2 cm) inserted to a depth of 40 cm to achieve sufficient contact; the Wenner configuration[7] was applied and the electrodes placed in the ground 1 m apart.

The resistivity values were clearly measurable and subject to interpretation. The excavation results confirm the extrapolation from electrical and magnetic prospecting, which are in close agreement. We have identified a number of rooms with courtyards enclosed by, in part, well-built walls of varying width, all forming an orthogonal pattern. The search for the town wall has so far proved fruitless.

GENERAL CONCLUSIONS

The use of electro-magnetic instruments at Hala Sultan Tekke throughout two seasons provided the following information of value for archaeological field work.

1. Investigation of known sites.

A. Depending on the purpose of the investigation, it is advisable to know where to start digging on an already defined site. A concentration of artifacts or changes in soil type, as indicated by a detector, may be of great assistance.

B. Time is usually short during rescue excavations. A detector could make possible more rapid digging.

2. Preliminary examination of the surface. After deciding where to start an excavation it is advisable to investigate the surface layer with a detector before starting to dig. It often happens that little attention is devoted to the surface layer; such a practice increases the risk of missing significant objects.

3. Investigation during ordinary excavations. A detector can provide valuable help in all excavations. The detector should be used only in conjunction with conventional and careful excavation in order to achieve satisfactory results. All excavations should be concluded by testing the surface with a detector.

A. The detector allows discovery of metal objects that are otherwise very difficult and sometimes impossible to find.

B. The detector indicates the presence of an artifact and allows definition of its size and shape before it is brought to light. Thus extreme care can be observed in the excavation, obviating possible damage to the buried object.

C. The detector can reveal the existence of metal objects inside or underneath walls, or below stone slabs.

4. The anticipation and discouragement of "treasure hunting". A surface survey can be performed with a detector near excavations or at other sites of archaeological interest before the advent of "treasure-hunters". If such individuals find artifacts there is an obvious risk that they will remove them, thereby destroying a valuable find context.

5. The possibility of discovering non-metal objects and features. Such items include ceramics of a certain thickness, including terracotta, mud bricks, ash, hornblende, chalky limestone, together with changes in soil type and structure which allow differentiation between strata and features.

6. The use of the VLF detectors discriminate modes can be of benefit on sites of archaeological interest, especially where the soil contains objects of iron, silver paper, or iron alloys of modern origin.

7. A possible disadvantage of the use of electromagnetic detectors lies in the (unfounded) expectation of discovering artifacts as soon as the instrument gives a positive reading. A detector should be regarded as a supplement to conventional excavation methods.

The hot and dry climate of Cyprus in summer did not hinder the resistivity survey; sufficient contact between the electrodes and the dry soil could nevertheless be attained. The stable soil humidity during the summer – rain being extremely rare – can be considered advantageous for electrical prospecting. The excavation results from different days can be compared without reference to varying humidity values.

ACKNOWLEDGEMENTS

I wish to thank Professor Paul Åström for making possible my participation in the excavations at Hala Sultan Tekke and for his helpful suggestions and comments.

APPENDIX

("Geophysical Prospecting at Hala Sultan Tekke, Cyprus – 'The Electro-Magnetic Survey' ").

The following tables reveal a more detailed description of the metal finds discovered (and not discovered) by the VLF detector during the 1979 survey.

Table 1 shows a synopsis of the metal finds from Area 8 South (the excavation area of the 1979 expedition) discovered by the VLF detector. Table 2 indicates three metal finds from Area 8 South which were not pointed out by the VLF detector. One fact was common to all three objects: The state of heavy corrosion. The three objects were later placed on the ground and tested individually with the VLF detector's search head close to them. The bronze fishing hook and the bronze pin gave no indication at all. The silver finger ring gave a faint indication. The heavy corrosion, which resulted in the loss of metal substance, seems to be the reason the VLF detector did not discover these objects.

Table 3 shows the results of the surface survey, which was executed over the areas surrounding Area 8 South.

Table 1. Metal objects discovered by VLF detector

Objects (total)	Size classes (cm)		Quantity	Maximum find depth (cm)
Bronze (34)	I	< 1,9	6	3
	II	2–3,9	12	17
	III	4–9,9	10	21
	IV	> 10	6	62
Copper (14)	I		7	6
	II		6	5
	III		1	surface find
	IV		0	–
Gold (22)	I		18	20
	II		4	20
	III		0	–
	IV		0	–
Iron (12)	I		2	surface finds
	III		5	5
	III		4	surface finds
	IV		1	10
Lead (72)	I		10	5
	II		55	28
	III		6	20
	IV		1	22
Silver (1)	I		0	–
	II		1	12
	III		0	–
	IV		0	
Uncertain (4)	I		0	–
	II		3	surface finds
	III		1	5
	IV		0	–

Table 1. Metal finds from Area 8 South discovered by the VLF detector

Find number	Object	Material	Size (cm) before cleaning	Excavated depth (cm)
N 1167A	Sling bullet	Lead	2.8x1.3	5
N 1168A	Net weight	Lead	3.4x0.9x0.2	3
N 1170A	Net weight	Lead	3.5x0.8x0.2	3
N 1173A	Spindle whorl	Lead	1.6x1.5	3
N 1179A	Sling bullet	Lead	3.4x1.5	9
N 1182A	Net weight	Lead	2.3x1.8x0.4	5
N 1183A	Escutcheon?	Lead	18.5x4.0x0.7	22
N 1184A	Dagger or spear head	Bronze	29.8x3.5x0.5	4
N 1185A	Cross-shaped cast channels?	Lead	3.8x2.9x1.8	5
N 1186	Sling bullet	Lead	3.1x1.5	3
N 1187	Sling bullet	Lead	3.4x1.9	11
N 1191	Sling bullet	Lead	3.6x1.9	15
N 1194	Sling bullet	Lead	3.2x1.6	16
N 1211	Sling bullet	Lead	3.8x1.6	5
N 1213	Round section piece	Bronze	2.2x0.9	3
N 1214	Net weight	Lead	2.6x1.0x0.5	3
N 1220	Dish with one handle	Bronze	26.0x5.0x0.3	52
N1221	Bowl	Bronze	13.3x5.0x0.5	52
N 1222	Jug with one handle	Bronze	16.0x14.0x0.1	52
N 1223	Sling bullet	Lead	3.4x1.7	28
N 1224	Arrow head	Bronze	7.6x1.8x0.4	17
N 1229	Dagger	Bronze	34.0x3.0x0.4	17
N 1231	Trident	Bronze	87.6x14.8x3.0	62
N 1232	Bolt	Bronze	6.2x1.2	17
N 1233	Flat strip	Bronze	2.9x0.5x0.2	17
N 1234	Scarab/Cartouche	Gold	2.3x1.6x0.9	15–20
N 1235	Bead, lined with caps	Gold	1.5x0.6	15–20
N 1236	–"–	Gold	1.7x0.4	15–20
N 1237	–"–	Gold	0.9x0.9	15–20
N 1238	–"–	Gold	1.6x0.5	15–20
N 1239	–"–	Gold	1.3x0.7	15–20
N 1240	–"–	Gold	1.7x0.5	15–20
N 1241	–"–	Gold	1.6x0.6	15–20
N 1242	–"–	Gold	1.2x0.8	15–20
N 1243	–"–	Gold	1.3x0.5	15–20
N 1244	–"–	Gold	1.9x0.6	15–20
N 1245	Cylindrical bead	Gold	0.6x0.5	15–20
N 1246	Bead, lined with caps	Gold	1.3x1.0	15–20
N 1247	Pendant	Gold	1.5x1.3x0.4	15–20
N 1248	Bead, lined with caps	Gold	1.8x0.7	15–20
N 1249	Discformed pendant	Gold	1.7x1.3	15–20
N 1250	Bead, lined with caps	Gold	1.2x0.9	15–20
N 1253	Net weight	Lead	1.9x1.5	On surface
N 1254	Sling bullet	Lead	3.4x1.6	6
N 1255	Sling bullet	Lead	3.5x1.7	6
N 1256	Bracelet	Bronze	7.9x5.2x0.9	c.10 cm beneath (an) ashlar block
N 1257	Escutcheon?	Bronze	4.5x1.7x0.6	On surface
N 1258	Sling bullet	Lead	3.2x1.6	On surface
N 1259	Net weight	Lead	2.7x2.2x0.2	On surface
N 1261	Net weight	Lead	1.6x1.4x1.0	On surface
N 1263	Handle?	Bronze	1.7x1.0x0.6	On surface
N 1264	Sling bullet	Lead	2.6x1.6	10
N 1265	Cylindrical weight	Lead	4.3x3.0	20

Find number	Object	Material	Size (cm) before cleaning	Excavated depth (cm)
N 1270	Coin	Copper	1.9x0.1	6
N 1282	Net weight	Lead	4.8x1.0x0.4	10
N 1290	Net weight	Lead	3.7x1.0x0.6	3
N 1301	Irregular fragment	Bronze	2.2x1.6x0.9	3
N 1302	Globular bead	Gold	1.1x0.9	5
N 1303	Spindle whorl	Lead	2.1x1.6	5
N 1304	Sling bullet	Lead	3.0x1.4	On surface
N 1305	Pin	Bronze	1.8x0.9	On surface
N 1306	Handle of a cup	Lead	3.4x1.4x0.5	8
N 1309	Sling bullet	Lead	3.3x1.5	On surface
N 1310	Net weight	Lead	2.0x1.9x0.3	On surface
N 1313	Sling bullet	Lead	3.5x1.7x1.4	6
N 1314	Spindle whorl	Lead	1.6x1.6	5
N 1315	Spindle whorl	Lead	1.3x1.2	3
N 1316	Button	Lead	2.1x1.3	5
N 1321	Oval sling bullet	Lead	3.3x2.0x1.5	3
N 1322	Sling bullet	Lead	3.8x1.5	3
N 1323	Sling bullet	Lead	4.1x1.5	3
N 1324	Sling bullet	Lead	4.0x1.6	3
N 1326	Sling bullet	Lead	3.5x1.6	4
N 1330	Sling bullet	Lead	3.4x1.6	4
N 1351	Bead lined with caps	Gold	2.1x0.6	15–20
N 1352	Bead lined with caps	Gold	2.0x0.6	15–20
N 1353	Solid finger-ring	Gold	2.6x0.4	15–20
N 1354	Bead lined with caps	Gold	1.3x1.2	15–20
N 1355	Arrow head	Bronze	7.6x2.1x0.5	20
N 1356	Arrow head	Bronze	8.0x1.9x0.4	21
N 1359	Rectangular piece	Silver	2.1x1.5x0.8	12
N 1365	Triangular piece	Bronze	2.1x1.0x1.1	5
N 1377	Irregular piece	Bronze	2.0x1.4x0.6	3
N 1377	Round piece	Bronze	1.3x0.4	3
N 1381	Mouse figurine	Bronze	3.6x1.2x1.4	7
N 1383	Net weight	Lead	3.8x1.2x0.5	5
No find number	Slag	Iron? Copper?	4.0x3.0	5
–"–	Slag	Copper	2.3x2.9	On surface
–"–	Slag	Copper	3.8x2.5	–"–
–"–	Slag	?	2.8x1.9	–"–
–"–	Slag	?	2.1x1.8	–"–
–"–	Slag	Copper	3.6x3.3	–"–
–"–	Nail	Iron	3.6x1.0	–"–
–"–	Irregular sheet	Lead	2.9x2.0	–"–
–"–	Irregular piece	Lead	2.2x1.7	–"–
–"–	Irregular piece	Lead	1.4x1.0	–"–
–"–	Irregular piece	Lead	1.1x0.9	–"–
–"–	Irregular sheet	Bronze	1.9x2.0	–"–
–"–	Irregular piece	Bronze	1.3x0.9	–"–
–"–	Irregular piece	Bronze	2.1x1.3	–"–
–"–	Irregular piece	Bronze	1.0x0.6	–"–

Table 2. Metal finds from Area 8 South not discovered by the VLF detector.

Find number	Object	Material	Size (cm)	Possible depth (cm)
N 1178A	Part of fishing hook	Bronze	2.5x0.3	5
N 1358	Fingerring	Silver	2.5x0.9x0.3	15
N 1363	Pin	Bronze	2.9x0.3	5

Table 3. Metal finds from Area 8 West, Area 21, Area 22 East, Area 22 North and Area 23 West discovered by the VLF detector.

Area 8 West:

Find number	Object	Material	Size (cm)	Excavated depth (cm)
N 1278	Sling bullet	lead	3.6x1.4	On surface
N 1279	Sling bullet	Lead	3.2x1.9	On surface

Area 21:

Find number	Object	Material	Size (cm)	Excavated depth (cm)
N 1311	Nail	Iron	4.8x0.9	On surface
N 1312	Pin	Iron	5.0x0.4	On surface
No find number	Irregular piece	Bronze	1.9x1.9	On surface
–"–	Spherical slag	Copper	D. 1.6	On surface

Area 22 East:

Find number	Object	Material	Size (cm)	Excavated depth (cm)
N 1181A	Round weight	Lead	5.1x3.6	11
N 1189	Sling bullet	Lead	3.6x1.5	5
N 1190	Pin	Bronze	4.9x0.7	On surface
N 1198	Sling bullet	Lead	3.3x1.6	4
N 1199	Sheet	Bronze	2.9x1.5x0.3	7
N 1200	Sling bullet	Lead	2.8x2.5	10
N 1201	Sling bullet	Lead	3.6x1.4	8
N 1202	Sling bullet (flattened)	Lead	3.8x2.0x0.9	5
N 1203	Rim fragment of vessel	Bronze	4.8x0.7x03	10
N 1204	Coin	Copper	2.4x0.2	5
N 1205	Drill?	Bronze	6.1x1.2	5
N 1206	Nail	Iron	11.9x0.5	10
N 1207	Button	Lead	1.7x0.9	5
N 1208	Escutcheon	Iron	2.3x1.4x1.2	5
N 1209	Lump	Lead	6.3x3.9x2.2	10
N 1210	Irregular piece	Lead	2.3x1.8x1.0	3
No find number	Irregular piece	Lead	2.5x2.2	On surface
–"–	–"–	Bronze	3.1x2.2	–"–
–"–	–"–	Bronze	2.2x2.1	–"–
–"–	–"–	Bronze	2.5x3.6	–"–
–"–	Slag	Copper	1.8x1.5	–"–
–"–	Slag	Copper	1.3x0.7	–"–

Area 22 North:

Find number	Object	Material	Size (cm)	Excavated depth (cm)
N 1196	Bi-conical bead	Lead	1.6x1.2	5
N 1268	Sling bullet	Lead	3.5x1.7	6
N 1271	Ingot?	Lead?	2.3x2.0x1.1	On surface
N 1272	Sling bullet	Lead	3.6x1.6	–"–
N 1273	Net weight	Lead	3.1x2.0x0.7	–"–
N 1274	Sling bullet	Lead	2.6x1.6	–"–
N 1275	Net weight	Lead	2.5x1.8x0.6	–"–
N 1276	Net weight	Lead	3.4x1.4x0.8	–"–
N 1277	Sling bullet	Lead	3.1x1.5	–"–
No find number	Sheet	Lead	4.0x1.6	–"–
–"–	Sheet	Lead	3.1x1.4	–"–
–"–	Sheet	Lead	2.7x2.5	–"–
–"–	Irregular piece	Lead	4.6x2.6	–"–
–"–	Irregular piece	Lead	2.8x1.3	–"–
–"–	Irregular piece	Lead	2.9x2.0	–"–
–"–	Nail	Iron	4.9x1.2	–"–
–"–	Nail	Iron	5.6x2.2	–"–
–"–	Nail	Iron	3.2x0.5	–"–
–"–	Slag	Copper	2.1x1.4	–"–
–"–	Slag	Copper	2.2x1.4	–"–
–"–	Slag	Copper	1.0x0.9	–"–
–"–	Slag	Copper	0.9x0.8	–"–
–"–	Slag	Copper	1.4x1.2	–"–
–"–	Slag	Iron	1.0x0.7	–"–
–"–	Slag	Iron	1.3x1.0	–"–

Area 23 West:

Find number	Object	Material	Size (cm)	Excavated depth (cm)
N 1174A	Nail	Iron	2.5x0.5	3
N 1177A	Net weight	Lead	3.8x1.5x1.1	10
No find number	Pin	Iron	3.4x1.6	On surface
–"–	Irregular piece	Bronze	4.1x3.5	–"–
–"–	Slag	Copper	6.0x4.8	–"–

NOTES

1. See the technical principles in R. C. V. Macario, "Discriminative Metal Detector," *Wireless World* (July 1978) 43–46.
2. P. M. Fischer, "The Use of a Metal Detector in Archaeology," *Opus Ath* 13, in press.
3. Colani and Aitken demonstrated the possibility of analysing different soil features with a PIM detector in C. Colani and M. J. Aitken, "A New Type of Locating Device. II-Field Trials," *Archaeometry* 9 (1966) 9–19.
4. See the article on lead sling bullets by P. Åström and I. Nicolaou in *Opus Ath* 13, in press.
5. No publication on electrical prospecting on Cyprus is known to the author at the time of printing.
6. R. E. Linington, in *Hala Sultan Tekke, Excavations 1972, Stud Med Arch* XLV:3 (Göteborg 1977) 13–27.
7. This is a system that measures resistivity by feeding an electrical current of known power into the ground through a pair of electrodes and measuring the voltage produced across a second pair of electrodes. See F. Wenner, "A Method of Measuring Earth Resistivity," *Bulletin of the U.S. Bureau of Standards* 12 (1916) 469.

40

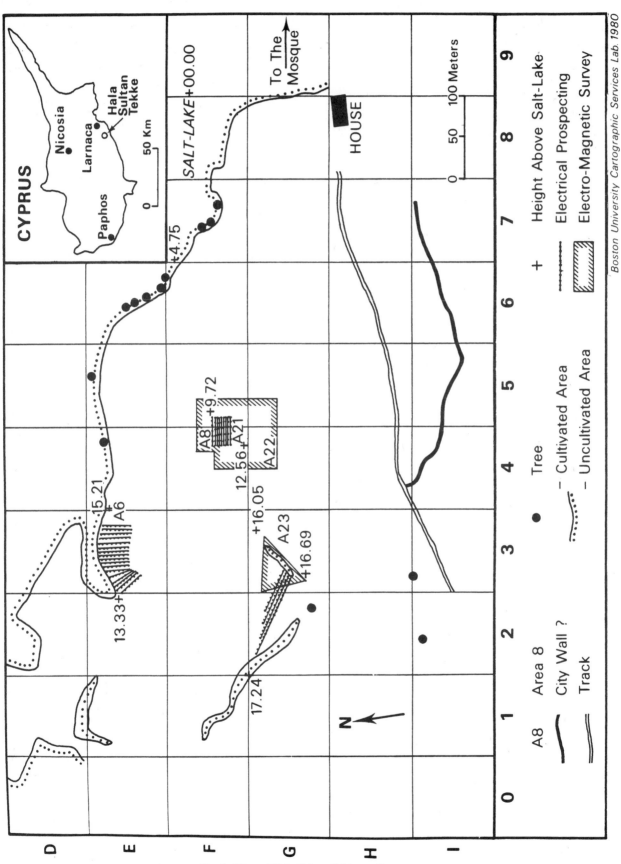

Fig. 1. Map of Hala Sultan Tekke on Cyprus.

Fig. 2. The detectors used at Hala Sultan Tekke, 1) Induction Balance "wide-scan" detector used mainly in 1978. 2) Very Low Frequency Discriminative detector. 3) Pulsed Induction detector used during the excavations in 1979.

Fig. 3. A bronze dish, bronze bowl, and bronze jug *in situ* between the skeleton's tube.

Fig. 4. Bronze trident in situ.

Fig. 5. Lead sling bullet in situ.

Fig. 6. Lead sling bullets.

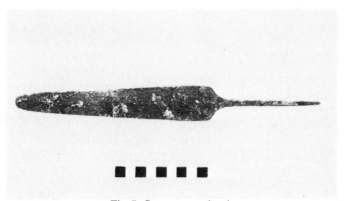

Fig. 7. Bronze spear head.

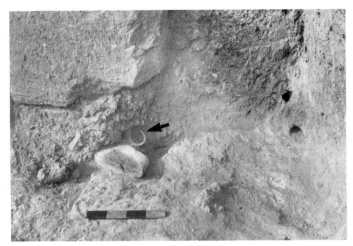

Fig. 8. Bronze bracelet beneath a stone slab.

Fig. 9. Gold bead.

Fig. 10. Lead weights, 750 g each.

ELECTRO-MAGNETIC DETECTORS
TECHNICAL PRINCIPLES AND FIELD TRIALS

INTRODUCTION

The basis of the surveying method is that of inducing an electro-magnetic field in the deposits under investigation. Irregularities in these deposits, especially materials of high conductivity, e.g. metal, cause eddy currents which in turn produce secondary electro-magnetic fields which can be measured by a receiver system on the instrument.[1] If the metal is ferromagnetic, its presence may have a decided effect on the inductance displayed by the coil and hence may vary the resonant frequency. Or if the metal acts as a short-circuited turn, the eddy currents induced in it will effect a resistive component into the impedance of which the coil is a part. This change in the resistive component has a similar (though less marked) effect on the resonant frequency.[2]

SOME TYPES AND THEIR CHARACTERISTICS

A lot of different instruments, with various modes of action, are available on the market (e.g. Metal Sensor, Three Stage Detection, Tunted-loop Oscillator with Crystal Filters, Beat Frequency detector, Two Oscillator Locator, Coin Finder and Single-Transistor used with A-M Radio.[3] Unfortunately the nomenclature is not internationally uniform, but there are four basic priciples of detector operation used in the most common modern instruments:

1. Beat Frequency Oscillator (BFO)
2. Induction Balance (IB) and Transmit-Receive (TR)
3. Pulsed Induction (PIM)
4. Very Low Frequency (VLF)

1. BFO

The BFO type of detector incorporates two high frequency oscillators. One of these, located in the control box is set at a fixed reference frequency of c. 120 kHz. The other, located in the search head, is variable. When in use it is set at a slightly higher frequency than the reference oscillator. This provides a continuous beat note. When the detector is passed over metal the frequency of the variable oscillator increases producing a faster beat and a higher note.[4] Most Beat Frequency detectors are characterised by their low cost, simplicity of use and construction and moderate depth penetration.

2. IB and TR

These detectors use a multi-coil system consisting of a transmitter and receiver coil located in the search head. The transmitter coil emits an electro-magnetic field and if there is no metal in the vicinity the field remains balanced with respect to the receiver coil; the frequency of the straightforward oscillator is c. 130 kHz. If the detector is passed over metal the receiver coil detects the imbalance caused by the metal distorting the field pattern. A voltage controlled oscillator gives about 70 Hz in "no metal" conditions which rises to about 500 Hz when metal is present.[5]

There are two distinct coil patterns. The first uses a small circular receiver coil located front of centre. It has a limited pick up area. The second uses an elongated receiver coil which stretches from the front to the back of the head, consequently the pick-up area is greater when searching. More area can be covered quickly with this type, but pin-pointing is not as clear cut.

The more sophisticated principle of IB/TR detectors offers definite advantages over the Beat Frequency detectors: Good sensitivity to small and large metallic objects, good depth penetration, good pin-pointing of the target object, good stability, greater sensitivity to non-ferrous metals such as gold, silver, bronze, copper and lead and adaptability for use on most terrains.

3. PIM[6]

A PIM detector uses a transmitter coil and receiver coil. The primary field transmitted into the ground consists of a direct current magnetic pulse lasting for about 1/2 millisecond. Pick up of the primary field is avoided by keeping the receiver circuitry inactive for the duration of the transmitter pulse. However if a metal object is linked by the transmitter field, eddy currents will be induced in the object at switch-off (as well as at switch-on). These eddy currents persist after switch-off, declining slowly for a good conductor and rapidly for a bad one. Thus in this case the receiver coil is linked by a secondary direct current magnetic field and a voltage is generated due to the changing magnetic linkage as this field decays.

The coil arrangement in this type of detector eliminates ground capacitance and allows the detector to be used effectively on all types of terrain and under water. Its sensitivity to all metals is good, especially iron. The depth penetration is very good, the pin-pointing of the target object is less efficient. A disadvantage, however, is the quite high power consumption.

4. VLF ("Discriminator")

Detectors using this principle are a recent development and work at a frequency between 2–25 kHz using a "single coil" search head arrangement. The essential difference between these types of detectors and the conventional BFO, IB/TR and IPM detectors is that VLF detectors measure the phase change in the current induced by the presence of a metal object rather than the amplitude change.[7] A detector based on the phase measuring priciple has the ability to indicate whether a hidden object, within the vicinity of the search coil, increases the magnetic field (ferro-magnetic) or decreases the magnetic field (diamagnetic).[8] Differences between, for example, buried iron or bronze and gold objects can be indicated. This type of detector is also called a "Discriminator".

VLF detectors have very good depth penetration and can be used effectively on all types of terrain.

FIELD TRIALS

Table 1. Advantages and disadvantages of different detectors.

Advantages	Disadvantages
BFO	
1. Simple to use	1. Moderate depth penetration
(2. Low cost)	2. Reduced sensitivity to small objects
	3. Less efficient tuning stability
IB/TR ("Pin-point")	
1. Good depth penetration	1. Very small pick-up area
2. Good sensitivity to all metals and to small objects	2. Slow coverage
3. Adaptability to most terrains	
4. Pin-point accuracy of location	
5. Good tuning stability	
6. Reacts negatively to small iron objects	
IB/TR ("Wide-scan")	
1. Good depth penetration	1. Slightly less accurate pin-pointing
2. Good sensitivity to all metals and to some non-metal objects[9]	
3. Adaptability to most terrains	
4. Quick coverage and greater pick-up area	
5. Good tuning stability	
6. Biased against small iron objects	
PIM	
1. Very good depth penetration	1. No clear cut pin-pointing
2. Good sensitivity to all metals, espec. iron and to some non-metal objects and features[9]	2. Slow indication of metal objects
3. Ignores ground effects – adaptability to all terrains	3. Slow coverage
4. Excellent for under water use	4. Reduced sensitivity to very small objects
5. Greater pick-up area	5. High power consumption
6. Good tuning stability	
7. Simple to use	
VLF ("Discriminator")	
1. Very good depth penetration	1. Quite complicated to use
2. Very good sensivity to all metals, to small objects and to some non-metal objects and features[9]	2. Reduced sensitivity to small objects and less efficient depth penetration when using in discriminate mode
4. Increased pick-up area	
5. Good pin-pointing	
6. Good tuning stability	
7. Discriminates against silver paper, iron and ferro-alloy when using in discriminate mode	

To give a definite answer about the depth penetration of the different detectors is quite difficult. There are so many effects to consider, e.g. metal oxides, the earth's magnetic fields, humidity, density and consistency, which influence the depth penetration. The best results are achieved in dry and compact soils containing a small amount of metal, especially ferrous oxides. Most metal objects, which have been buried for a long time, build up a sphere of metal oxides around them which makes their detection easier.

In table 2 an attempt has been made to compare depth penetrations of each of the different types of detector. The lower values correspond to a metal object the size of a Swedish crown (D. 2,5 cm). The higher values correspond to a metal object with a diameter greater than 30 cm.

Table 2. Approximate depth penetrations of different detectors.

Approximate depth penetration
(in cm)

BFO:	10–20/40–50
IB/TR:	20–30/50–75
PIM:	20–30/75–100
VLF:	30–40/75–100

These values refer to the most common detectors on the market with search head diameters of 20–25 cm. The sensitivity of a search head varies with size. The larger the search head the greater the sensitivity to big objects. A 200 cm depth penetration is possible. However, when a large coil dimension is involved, the maintenance of the precise coil alignment becomes difficult; the sensitivity of the instrument is therefore reduced and consequently the location of small objects is no longer possible.[10] A small search head has a very good sensitivity to very small objects but the depth penetration is insufficient. Therefore a search head diameter of 20–25 cm on a sophisticated detector is able to indicate shallowly buried objects a few mm in size and big objects down to about a depth of 100 cm.

NOTES

1. R. E. Linington, *Technical Introduction to Prospecting Problems* (Rome 1979), 26–27.
2. D. G Fink and J. M. Carrol, *Standard Handbook for Electrical Engineers* (New York 1968), sec.28, 64.
3. J. Marcus, *Guidebook of Electronic Circuits* (New York 1974), 496–499.
4. D. E. O'N. Waddington, "Metal Detector", *Wireless World* (April 1977), 45–48.
5. ETI Project Team, "IB Metal Locator MK2", *Electronics Today International* (February 1978), 32–35.
6. For fuller discussion see:
   M. J. Aitken, *Physics and Archaeology* (Oxford 1974), 196–198.
   C. Colani, "A New Type of Locating Device. I– the Instrument", *Archaeometry* 9 (1966), 3–8.
   E. I. Foster, "Further Developments of the Pulsed Induction Metal Detector", *Prospezioni Archeologiche 3* (1968), 95–99.
7. See C-Scopes booklet about VLF detectors, C-Scope, Ashford, Kent, England.
8. R. C. V. Macario, "Discriminative Metal Detector", *Wireless World* (July 1978), 43.
9. Such items included ceramics, ash, limestone together with changes in soil type and structure which allow differentiation between strata and featurers (PIM, VLF).
10. M. S. Tite, *Methods of Physical Examination in Archaeology* (Seminar Press, London – New York 1972), 33–34.

THE USE OF A SOIL CONDUCTIVITY METER (SCM) AT HALA SULTAN TEKKE, CYPRUS

INTRODUCTION

During the 1980 excavation season of the Late Cypriote Bronze Age town at Hala Sultan Tekke a survey with a Soil Conductivity Meter (SCM) was performed by the writer. The instrument used was a "Pipe Seeker 5" made by Compass Electronics Inc., Oregon, U.S.A. This type of electro-magnetic instrument[1] consists of a tracer (transmitter) coil and a receiver coil mounted on the same rigid shaft 1 m apart. The plane of the tracer coil is vertical whereas that of the receiver coil is horizontal (Fig. 1). Signals indicated by the receiver unit (audially or visually) are due to "disturbances" from eddy currents and magnetizations caused by metal objects and other man-made features or minor geological structures. The purpose of this survey was to test the applicability of the SCM at Hala Sultan Tekke and to compare it with other technical devices.

Fig. 1. The Soil Conductivity Meter.

RESULTS

An area of some 4000 m² was investigated holding the SCM at the same distance from the surface in a horizontal position and walking along gridlines 1 m apart. In three places distinct and defined signals were obtained. All three indications were obtained in places where the excavation had reached deeper layers. A test excavation made at the position of the first indication resulted in the discovery of a concentration of mudbricks a few decimeters below the surface. A second test excavation was done in the area of the second indication and disclosed a disturbance in the floor of a room containing a stone wall c. 10 cm below surface belonging probably to an earlier period of the town. Due to lack of time, no follow-up has been done concerning the third indication.

The signal readings obtained from surface layers were ambiguous and indistinct, extending over areas of at least 5 x 5 m. But all the test trenches, which were dug in places indicated by a later ground-penetrating radar survey and leading mainly to the discovery of walls, also lay in areas indicated by the SCM. No metal finds were indicated by the SCM.

CONCLUSIONS

The SCM was not a substitute for electrical resistivity measurements or magnetic prospecting.[2] It had of course the advantage of simplicity and a good surveying speed (c. 1 km/h) but the disadvantage seems to be its ability to detect only shallow buried features thereby providing an indistinct indication of these features given the conditions at Hala Sultan Tekke.

NOTES

1. For a more detailed description of the basic technical principles and for different applications see M. J. Aitken, *Physics and Archaeology* (Oxford 1974) 191–193, M. Howell, "A Soil Conductivity Meter", *Archaeometry* 9 (1966) 20–23 and M. S. Tite and C. Mullins, "Electromagnetic Prospecting on Archaeological Sites using a Soil Conductivity Meter", *Archaeometry* 12 (1970) 97–104.
2. See also Aitken (op. cit. in note 1) 191.

SUBSURFACE INTERFACE RADAR SURVEY AT HALA SULTAN TEKKE, CYPRUS

by

Peter M. Fischer, Sven G. W. Follin and Peter Ulriksen

INTRODUCTION

In July/August 1980 as a result of cooperation between the Departments of Ancient Culture and Civilization, University of Gothenburg, and Engineering Geology, Lund Institute of Technology, a Subsurface Interface Radar (SIR) survey was performed at Hala Sultan Tekke, Cyprus, using a SIR-system built by Geographical Survey System Incorporated (GSSI), Hudson N. H., U.S.A. (Fig. 1)

The purpose of the radar survey was an attempt to trace subsurface structures of archaeological value in support of the excavations at Hala Sultan Tekke directed by Professor Paul Åström.

At the same site in 1972 a proton magnetometer survey was made by R. E. Linington, Lerici Foundation, Rome;[1] in 1979 electrical resistivity measurements and during the seasons 1978–1980, electromagnetic probes were carried out by P. M. Fischer.[2]

INSTRUMENTATION

A Subsurface Interface Radar (SIR) operates on the principle that electro-magnetic energy, in the shape of a very short pulse, is transmitted into the ground. On its way through the soil, part of the energy is reflected against interfaces and objects, while the rest proceeds to greater depths, being attenuated in proportion to the travelled distance.

By measuring the time between transmitted and reflected signals, the shape of interfaces and location of buried objects can be surveyed. If the pulse-propagation velocity is known, the depth of the reflectors can be calculated,

The transmitted pulse and the reflections are displayed on a cathode-ray tube (CRT) in the control unit and on a graphic recorder. While the CRT only displays the scan in progress, the graphic recorder displays all previous scans, so that the structure of the interfaces can easily be interpreted as can the location of objects in the soil.

The operation of the graphic recorder is as follows. A belt with two styluses moves across electrosensitive paper. The stylus is fed by the amplified incoming signal and when this reaches a preselected threshold, the surface of the paper is burned off, leaving a dark trace. The next time a stylus comes to the left side of the paper, a new signal is displayed and the paper is advanced, so that the signals are lined up side by side. The antenna has been simultaneously moved a short distance, so the new signal comes from a new location. The operation is explained by Figure 2.[3] (Note that the ground surface is a reference and always flat, as shown in Fig. 2.)

The signals can also be recorded on a tape-recorder. This makes it possible to process the signals in the laboratory so that the optimum results can be obtained (Fig. 3).

Antennas are available for different frequencies, presently 80, 120, 300, 400, 500 and 900 MHz. Generally the low-frequency antennas are larger and have a greater penetration and smaller resolution than the high-frequency antennas.

The antennas are connected to the control-unit with a 30 m long cable, making it possible to survey 60 m long continuous profiles.

The entire system was powered by a 2 kW gasoline generator.

PROPERTIES AFFECTING THE OPERATION

The two most important features of a SIR-system are the resolution and the penetration. Both are dependant on instrument properties and terrain conditions.

The resolution is commonly said to be half a wavelength, meaning that a sphere with that diameter can be detected. The depth to a horizontal interface can be detected with an accuracy of about one tenth of a wavelength.

The wavelength λ, is connected to the frequency f, and the velocity of propagation v, by the well-known expression:

$$v = \lambda \cdot f \tag{1}$$

The frequency is an instrument property and the velocity is a terrain property. The velocity is usually expressed as the relative dielectric constant ε_r which is related to the propagation velocity in vacuum c (c = $3 \cdot 10^8$ m/s) and in the soil v by the expression

$$\varepsilon_r = (\frac{c}{v})^2 \qquad (2)$$

A logarithmic relation between the relative dielectric constant and the volumetric water-content of the soil has been proposed.[4] As the water content increases so does the relative dielectric constant, which means that the propagation velocity decreases together with the wavelengh.

Briefly, it can be said that the possibility to detect small objects increases as the water content increases.

The penetration of the SIR-system is dependant on the sensitivity of the receiver and the attenuation A in the soil. The latter is a function of frequency f, relative dielectric constant ε_r and electrical conductivity σ in the following relation.[5]

$$A = 12.863 \cdot 10^{-8} \cdot f \cdot \varepsilon_r^{\frac{1}{2}} \cdot$$
$$\cdot ((\tan^2 \delta + 1) - 1)^{\frac{1}{2}} \, dB/m \qquad (3)$$

where

$$\tan \delta = \frac{\sigma}{2 \pi \cdot f \cdot \varepsilon_0 \cdot \varepsilon_r} \qquad (4)$$

$$\varepsilon_0 = 8.85 \cdot 10^{-12} \, (F/m)$$

The sensitivity of a SIR-system is described in dB/m, being 10 times the logarithm of the ratio between reflected and transmitted pulse. A survey with different ground penetrating radar-systems has been performed and sensitivity ranging from -67 to -159 dB has been shown.[6] The GSSI-system operated in this article is reported to have a sensitivity of -110 dB. This means that the transmitted pulse can be up to 10^{11} times greater than the minimum detected reflection. In practice however the signal is not only attenuated but also scattered and reflected against the groundsurface. It is therefore advisable to calculate with a sensitivity in the order of 40–60 dB.[7]

In dry sand penetrations of 30–40 m have been obtained. At Hala Sultan Tekke the soil is rather dry, but it can be rolled to a diameter of 1.5 mm if some water is added. This indicates a rather high clay-content and a correspondingly high electric conductivity, which will make the penetration very poor, in the order of 1–2 m when using the 400 MHz antenna. However, the expected depth of the archaeological structures was not in excess of operation.

METHOD OF OPERATION

The 400 MHz and the 900 MHz antenna were used at Hala Sultan Tekke. The antennas were towed by hand at a velocity corresponding to a slow walk (Fig. 4). This made it possible to avoid the operation of the tape-recorder, which is necessary if greater speeds are desired. In that way the result was available immediately, which proved to be of great value. With the tape-recorder the antennas could have been moved at a velocity of about 20 km/h.

Parts of the survey were performed with the antennas towed in a grid-system with markers every 5 m. These markers were electronically transferred to the graphic recorder for later identification. The distance between grid-lines is a trade-off between desired detection probability and production-rate. Since the radiation cone in the lateral direction has a top-angle of about 60°,[8] a grid-line spacing of 2 m will give a complete coverage at the same *depth*, which is also supposed to be the maximum penetration in the area. Later in the survey it was expanded to 4 m due to limited time and even later we went over to "wild-cat" surveying, i.e. moving the antenna in a random manner. The entire survey was performed along east-west grid-lines. Areas of special interest were investigated in complementary directions too.

RESULTS

In order to test the proper function of the radar equipment, investigations were done on the top of baulks containing walls: Clearly interpretable echoes corresponding to the underlying walls were obtained on the graphic recorder. The 400 MHz antenna was preferable to the 900 MHz antenna, since the higher frequency was more attenuated in the high-conductivity soil (Fig. 5, 6).

A survey of some 5000 m^2 was performed in Area 8 South – the area of the present excavations – in areas surrounding Area 8 South and in the north-eastern part of the town near the salt lake (see the map in Fig. 7). Significant radar echoes were directly marked on the ground. 12 test trenches were dug in places where the most significant radar echoes were obtained (see table 1).

In test trenches 1 and 2, walls were discovered. A very interesting fact was that the same type of wall has been excavated in Area 8 and Area 8 South and this seems to suggest that this wall borders a street through the town, connecting Area 8 with Area 22 to the south. Along an imaginary line connecting the walls from test trenches 1, 2 and the wall in Area 8 South more similar radar echoes were obtained. Continuing this imaginary line to the north, the structures discovered in test trenches 5 and 9 and in the most northeastern part of the town in test trenches 6 and 7 are perhaps the same wall bordering the street to the salt lake.

Table 1. The results from 12 test trenches.

Test trench (m)	Discovered structure	Appr. depth of structure (m)	Appr. width of structure (m)	Spec. remarks
1 (2x1) Fig. 8[10]	wall	0.3	0.8	
2 (2x1) Fig. 9	wall	0.4	≧ 0.5	In line with the wall of test trench 1.
3 (2x1) Fig. 10	blocks of stones (wall?)	0.2	0.8	
4 (2x1) Fig. 11	wall	0.3	≧ 0.3	
5 (2x1) Fig. 12	blocks of stones (wall)	0.5	≧ 0.4	Test trench contained large pithos sherds.
6 (2x1) Fig. 13	walls	0.2	≧ 0.4; ≧ 0.7	
7 (2x1) Fig. 14	walls	0.3	≧ 0.3; ≧ 0.3	
8 (2x1) Fig. 15	–	–	–	Clay soil; filled pit?
9 (2x1) Fig. 16	wall	0.5	≧ 0.4	
10 (2x1) Fig. 17	heap of stones	0.6	≧ 0.2	
11 (1x1) Fig. 18	wall	0.3	≧ 0.3	Beneath the floor of a courtyard belonging to to an earlier period.
12 (followed a disturbance in the floor of a room) Fig. 19	blocks of stones	0.1	?	Beneath the floor of a room, part of an earlier period? Tomb? Metal finds.

With respect to a suspected architectural structure, the negative digging results from test trench 8 can perhaps be explained by a nearby heap of earth which could have disturbed the radar antenna, giving a wrong indication. But the radar echo obtained is not similar to any other echoes in the survey. Further excavations could be valuable. A pit filled with clay soil and an underlying structure has been considered a possibility.

Another striking result is the discovery of the end of a wall in test trench 11 situated beneath the central courtyard of Area 8 South and belonging to an earlier period of the town. It was possible to follow the course of this wall to the east on open spaces where it was practicable to use the radar antenna. The length of this wall is approximately 11 m, a view supported by excavations to the east revealing what is possibly the other end of the wall.

Test trench 12 followed a disturbance in the floor of a room leading to the discovery of large blocks of stones. Metal finds, such as an arrow head, a bronze nail and a bronze head (?), were discovered by a recently developed Very Low Frequency detector[9] together with a faience scarab between the blocks of stones. The possibility of the presence of a tomb has been discussed. Lack of time prevented further excavations.

A baulk not containing any walls was chosen to test the ability of the radar to differentiate between different archaeological layers. It has not been possible to interpret the radar echoes with respect to the different layers (Fig. 20).

Near subsurface, minor metal artifacts gave spectacular "ringing" on the graphic recorder as shown in Figure 21.

CONCLUSIONS

The use of a Subsurface Interface radar system has been shown to be of value for archaeological field work.[11] The possibility of obtaining directly interpretable radar results concerning the near subsurface is of special interest for archaeologists and makes the method in this way superior to magnetic and electrical investigations, which need time consuming data processing not possible in the field.

The SIR-system can be used for a rapid large scale survey, revealing areas with architectural remains and "empty" spaces and for the detection of such minor structures as e.g. single walls with their courses. Near subsurface, minor metal artifacts have been indicated too. The depth of the deepest structure revealed by the SIR-system was 60 cm, but the maximum penetration when using the 400 MHz antenna is assumed to be c. 2 m in spite of the poor radar penetration at Hala Sultan Tekke, where the soil has a rather high clay-content. However, the expected depth of the archaeological structures was not in excess of the penetration.

It is our impression that the observed echoes should be marked in the terrain as soon as they are detected. This will facilitate the location of echoes in the excavation phase. The tedious operation of establishing grid-lines or the expense of having an automatic position system increases the ability to make a pre-excavation map of the area, but there will always, however, be difficulties in pinpointing the location of an echo in the terrain from a map. It will never be easier to find the spot than it is when you have just passed it. This is also a good way of utilizing the radar's capability of producing a final result directly in the field. Grid-lines assure that the entire area is covered but they have the disadvantage of being linear. Consequently they can run parallel with buried walls and thus make detection difficult or impossible. "Wild-cat" surveying is easier and faster to perform and does not suffer from the problem of parallelism.

The best operational procedure is probably to start out with a "wild-cat" survey of the entire area in question and then concentrate on the parts where a number of echoes are found. In these parts grid-lines can be established in an optimum manner so as to avoid parallellism, since the marks show the possible linearity of the structures. In both phases it is of primary importance to mark the echoes as soon as they are found.

NOTES

1. R. E. Linington, in "Hala Sultan Tekke, Excavations 1972", *Studies in Mediterranean Archaeology* XLV:3 (Göteborg 1977), 13–27.
2. P. M. Fischer, "Geophysical Prospecting at Hala Sultan Tekke, Cyprus", *Journal of Field Archaeology* (Boston Univ. 1980) in press.
3. See L. Bjelm, H. Bruch and P. Ulriksen, *Blocklokalisering med Georadar vid Motorvägsbygget E-4, Brohagen–Sille i D-Län* (Lunds Tekniska Högskola 1979).
4. L. F. Silva, F. V. Schultz and I. T. Zalusky, "Electrical Methods of Determining Soil Moisture Content", *LARS* Information Note 112174 (Purdue Univ. 1975).
5. R. M. Morey, "Continuous Subsurface Profiling by Impulse Radar", *American Society of Civil Engineering* (Aug. 1974).
6. A. P. Annan and I. L. Davis, *Radar Range Analysis for Geological Materials*, Resource Geophysics and Geochemistry Revision, Project 750037 (1977).
7. R. Vickers, L. Dolphin and D. Johnson, *Archaeological Investigations at Chaco Canyon Using a Subsurface Radar*, (Stanford Univ. 1976).
8. R. M. Morey, *Feasibility Study of Electromagnetic Subsurface Profiling* (GSSI, Oct. 1972).
9. The detector used was a VLF 3000 ADC made by C-Scope, Ashford, Kent, G.B.
10. The arrows on the photographs in fig. 8–19 indicate north. The arrows on the graphic recorder papers show the surveying direction (from or to east, north); the surface is up.
11. Cf. R. Vickers and R. Bollen, *Results of a Radar Survey for the Oswego West Side Sewer Project* (Stanford Univ. 1978) and L. Dolphin, W. Beatty and J. Tanzi, "Radar Probing of Victoria Peak, New Mexico", *Geophysics*, Vol. 43, No. 7 (December 1978), 1441–1448.

Fig. 1. The SIR-system as used at Hala Sultan Tekke.
A: Kabel vinch, B: Radar control unit,
C: Voltage converter, D: Graphic recorder,
E: 900 MHz antenna, F: 400 MHz antenna.

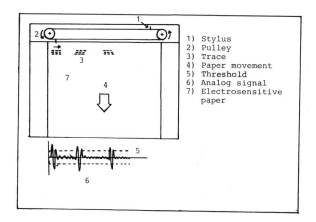

1) Stylus
2) Pulley
3) Trace
4) Paper movement
5) Threshold
6) Analog signal
7) Electrosensitive
   paper

Fig. 2. The operation principle of the graphic recorder.

Fig. 3. The SIR-system with a tape-recorder.

Fig. 4. The SIR-system with the 400 MHz antenna in use.

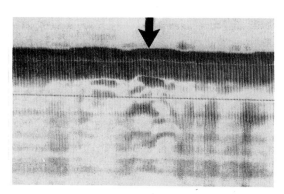

Fig. 5. A buried wall indicated by the 400 MHz antenna.

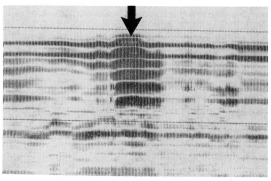

Fig. 6. The same wall (see Fig. 5) indicated by the 900 MHz antenna.

53 Fig. 5   900 MHz instead of 400 MHz
53 Fig. 6   400 MHz instead of 900 MHz

54

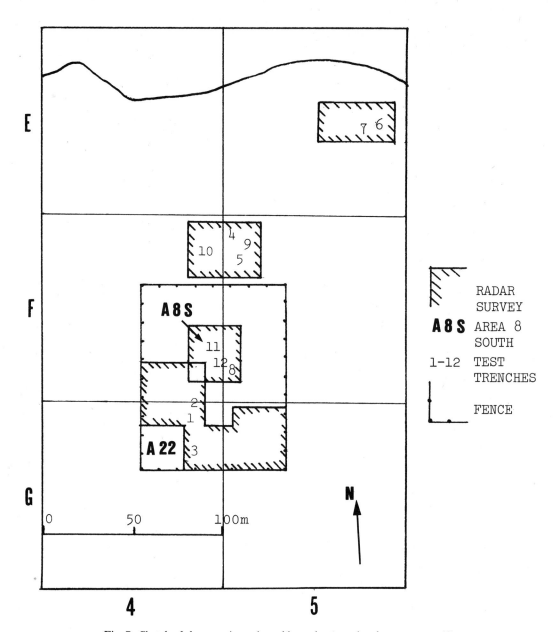

Fig. 7. Sketch of the areas investigated by radar (see also the map on p. 40)

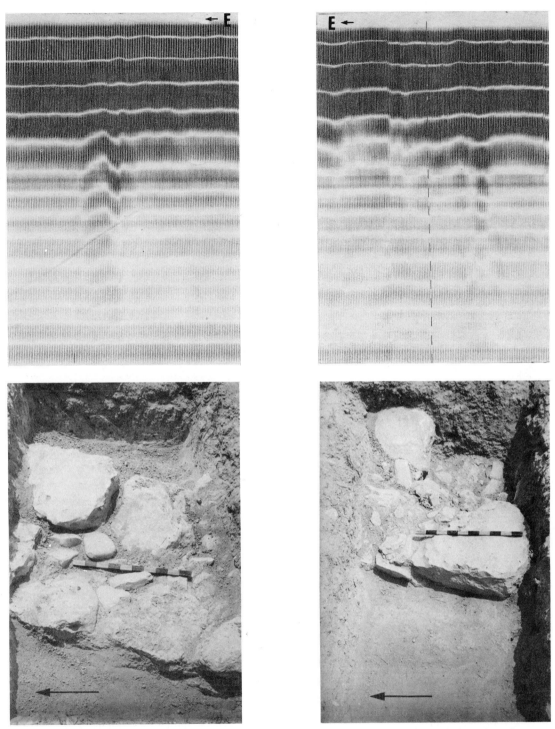

Fig. 8. Test trench 1 with the radar echoes.　　Fig. 9. Test trench 2 with the radar echoes.

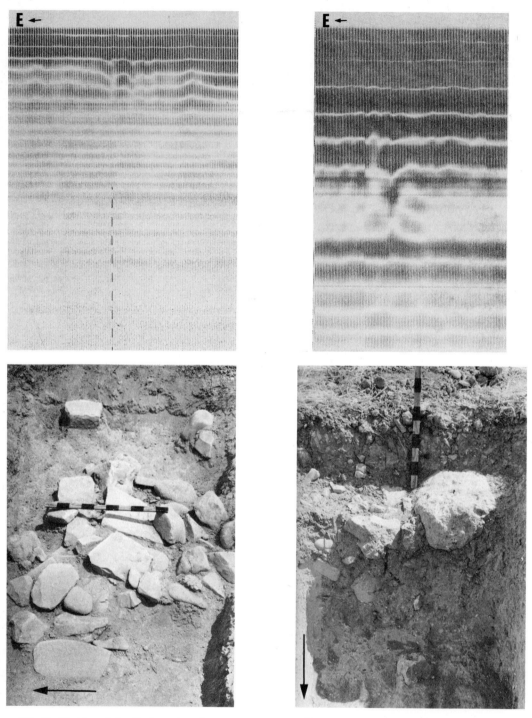

Fig. 10. Test trench 3 with the radar echoes.   Fig. 11. Test trench 4 with the radar echoes.

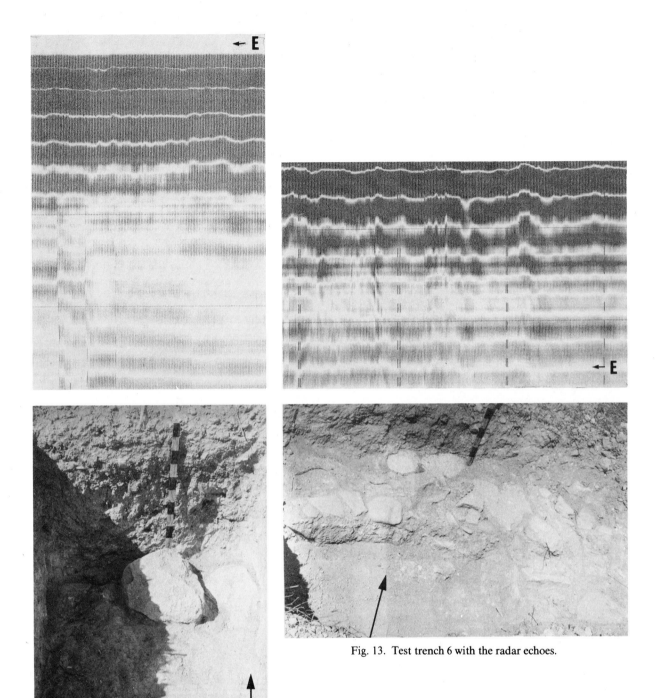

Fig. 13. Test trench 6 with the radar echoes.

Fig. 12. Test trench 5 with the radar echoes.

58

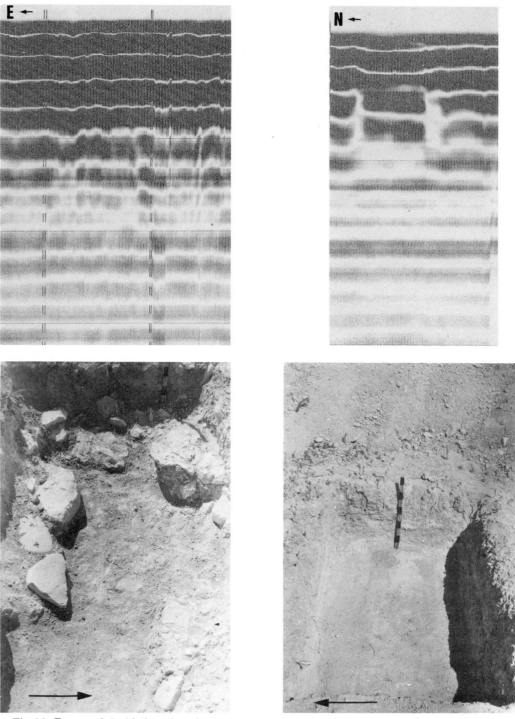

Fig. 14. Test trench 7 with the radar echoes.

Fig. 15. Test trench 8 with the radar echoes.

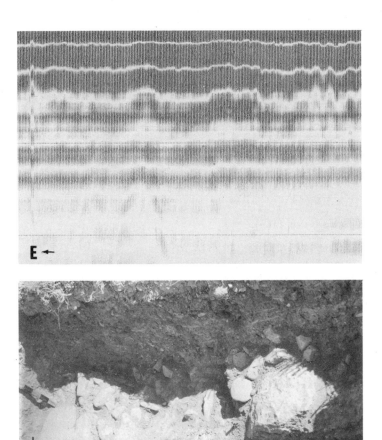

Fig. 16. Test trench 9 with the radar echoes.

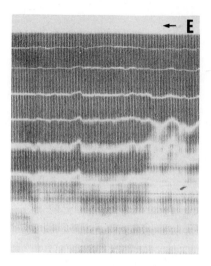

Fig. 17. Test trench 10 with the radar echoes.

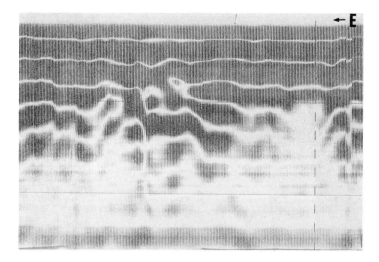

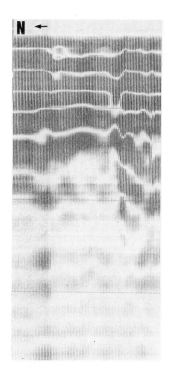

Fig. 18. Test trench 11 with the radar echoes.

Fig. 19. Test trench 12 with the radar echoes.

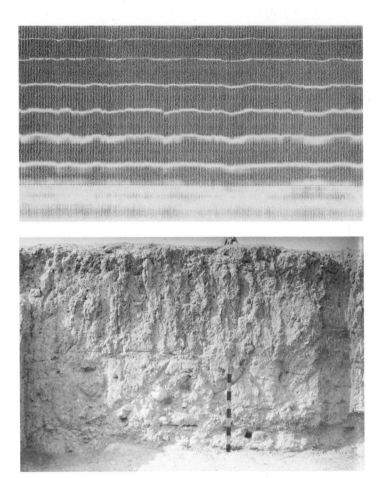

Fig. 20. Archaeological layers and their non-significant echoes.

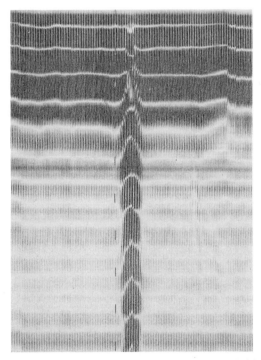

Fig. 21. Typical "ringing" caused by a minor metal object.

GENERAL DISCUSSION

1. THE DENTAL INVESTIGATIONS

The diagnostic methods used in this archaeological investigation were X-rays, the microscope and direct inspection. The use of X-rays on dental-archaeological material should be considered routine. Pathological changes, which are sometimes not detectable by direct inspection, can with X-Rays be observed with accuracy. The histopathological investigation simply confirmed the diagnosis made by direct inspection but should be seen only as a method of checking dubious diagnoses of pathological changes in ancient jaws and teeth, e.g. caries and mineralisation defects.

2. PROSPECTING

The prospecting methods used by the writer at Hala Sultan Tekke were electrical and electro-magnetic.

A. Electrical prospecting:
This is a method for investigation of known sites measuring geophysical variations and leading to a reasonably detailed plan of the site, at least under stable humidity conditions e.g. the Hala Sultan Tekke summer. With electrical prospecting it was possible to obtain a more detailed interpretation than that obtained by previous magnetic surveys in the same area. Other advantages are the fairly low cost of the equipment and the moderate cost of use. A disadvantage, however, is the slow pace. The depth penetration of this method when using the "Wenner" configuration with four electrodes, 1 m apart, and driven in to a depth of 40 cm, was 1–2 m.

B. Electro-magnetic prospecting
a) Electro-magnetic detectors
The electro-magnetic detectors used were Beat Frequency Oscillator (BFO), The Induction-Balance/Transmit-Receive (IB/TR), the Pulsed Induction (PIM) and the Very Low Frequency (VLF-discriminator).

The electro-magnetic detectors were of considerable value during the investigation of the known site at Hala Sultan Tekke. They were used for a surface survey and during the excavations mainly for the discovery and pin-pointing of metal objects which resulted, *inter alia*, in the discovery of a rich shaft grave. The detectors indicated the presence of artifacts and allowed definition of their sizes and shapes before they were reached by digging tools. Thus, extreme care could be observed in the excavation, avoiding possible damage to the buried objects. The IB/TR, PIM and VLF-discriminator showed the possibility of discovering non-metal objects. Such items included ceramics of a certain thickness, including terracotta, mud bricks, ash, hornblended and chalky limestones. The PIM and VLF-discriminator also indicated changes in soil type and structure which allowed differentiation between strata and features. The best results were obtained by the VLF-discriminator, which could differentiate between metals before the objects were brought to surface. The VLF was also the most complicated to use.

The cost of these devices is moderate and the cost of use and maintenance very low. The surveying speed is moderate and maximum depth penetration for the PIM and VLF is c. 1 m and a few decimetres less for the BFO and IB/TR.

A possible disadvantage of the use of electro-magnetic detectors is the temptation to dig for artifacts as soon as the instrument gives a positive reading. These detectors should be regarded only as supplements to conventional and careful excavation methods.
b) Soil Conductivity Meter (SCM)
The SCM detected only shallow buried features thereby providing an indistinct indication of these features, giving a fairly difficult interpretation. The advantages of the moderate cost of the equipment, the very low cost of use and the good surveying speed do not compensate for its disadvantages. The SCM could not be seen as a substitute for electrical or magnetic prospecting.
c) Subsurface Interface Radar (SIR)
The use of a SIR-system was shown to be of value during the survey at Hala Sultan Tekke. The SIR-system can be used for a rapid large-scale survey, revealing areas with architectural remains and "empty" spaces as well as for the detection of such minor structures as e.g. single walls and their courses or near subsurface minor metal artifacts.

The advantage of obtaining directly interpretable radar results concerning the near subsurface is of special interest for archaeologists and makes this method in this way superior to the magnetic and electrical investigations performed at Hala Sultan Tekke, which needed time-consuming data evaluations.

High moisture content of the soil, e.g. clay rich soil, or wet limestone often means high radar attenuation, reducing the depth penetration. When using the 400 MHz antenna the maximum depth penetration is assumed to be c. 2 m in spite of the rather high clay content of the soil at Hala Sultan Tekke.

Disadvantages of this method are the extremely high cost of the equipment and the heavy and large instruments, which make transportation quite difficult. If it was possible to build a cheaper and lighter radar system the method would be even more superior to other prospecting methods and could be used routinely when soil conditions permitted.

At an archaeological site modern geophysical methods can reveal information about what lies beneath the surface, in advance of excavation. Usually geophysical methods are nondestructive – less informed excavation can diminish or destroy the evidence. Therefore it is desirable to use suitable geophysical methods before starting excavation and during excavations to get maximum information about what lies beneath.